# Jamaica's Gifts to the World

# Jamaica's Gifts to the World

by Lloyd Eubank-Green

First published in Jamaica 2010 by
Ian Randle Publishers
11 Cunningham Avenue, Box 686
Kingston 6
www.ianrandlepublishers.com


ISBN: 978-976-637-4143



Cover and book design by Ian Randle Publishers

# TABLE OF CONTENTS

# PREFACE

This book is about building individual and national confidence. It is about answering questions concerning the part Jamaicans play and continue to play in the larger world forum. The aim of this book is to help you to live the life which perhaps, until now, you have only imagined for yourself. Its strategy is to give you the tools to create that life so that however great the obstacles you may meet, you will know that you have what it takes to surmount them.

It is now clear that each of us has something special about us. Every individual has a unique vision, a meaning and purpose to his or her life, with which we can be the most successful, the most fulfilled, and the happiest. The discovery and fulfillment of that unique vision is our life's purpose that brings with it the greatest happiness for us and all the persons in our surroundings.

Some of these selections might seem unremarkable to some readers but they were used to represent what is possible in that particular context. Of necessity, the accounts are short, so readers are encouraged to do further research. Indeed, with the help of the internet and books, students can do further research on most of the selections.

In this manuscript, Jamaican is taken to mean someone who is born and bred in Jamaica, a Jamaican who grew up in a foreign country, someone who was born in a foreign country of Jamaican parentage, or someone who has become a naturalized Jamaican. If you do know of any, who you think merits being included in a book of this nature, please do not hesitate to contact the author at: Lloyd@colis.com.

May this work touch you deeply, not only in your mind, but also in your heart; may it inspire you in such a way that you will rise and turn your dreams into reality – a reality that will help you, your surroundings and the world to be a better place.

Lloyd Eubank-Green,

# ACKNOWLEDGEMENTS

This book owes its existence to a number of persons and organizations. To my wife, Dr Pauline Williams-Green, who, with the rest of the family, acted as editor and motivator; the Jamaica National Building Society Foundation for their invaluable assistance with the printing, publication and public relations; Revd Dr Webster Edwards who advised me to write the book; Cloreth Greene and Petra-Gaye Morris who typed the manuscript; Dawn Williams for her tremendous input; Ricky Richardson and John Edwin Burke for their constant encouragement.

# ACADEMIA

# CARLENE CAMPBELL

She was told by the course director at London's South Bank University that she could not pursue the Masters of Science in Engineering because she did not have the basic qualifications. However, she did have the basic qualification to pursue a Masters of Science, having done a University of Technology (UTECH) degree in Computer Studies but that was nothing near to Engineering.

Carlene was not easily put-off. She was determined and focused. She went to England to be interviewed for entrance to the course at London's South Bank University. When the course director explained the situation to her, she looked him squarely in the eyes and said: 'I came all the way from Jamaica to do this course and you want to send me back?' The course director relented and accepted her on the course for two weeks on the understanding that she would identify an alternative course that she could manage. At the start of the course Carlene was totally dumbfounded; she did not understand a word.

Every week the course director would come to the class and ask for transfer letters to other courses but Carlene simply ignored him. She borrowed books, bought more books and laboured hard. Soon she discovered that other persons were also having trouble coping with the work. She continued to work hard.

Later on, she came top in the Director's course and got her Masters of Science in 2004. Yet, she had no engineering background.

# DANIEL THOMAS

Ardenne schoolboy Daniel Thomas was speechless when the principal informed him in September 2004 that he had won the Caribbean Examinations Council (CXC) award for most outstanding performance in the sciences in the region. The young man had scored distinctions in all 10 subjects.

The highly religious young man had this to say: 'I don't think I am really what you call a science student, and even though I did well in all three – Physics, Chemistry and Biology – I did not think that I would get the highest in the Caribbean, that never crossed my mind'.

Although he did not consider himself a 'science student', Daniel did choose the sciences because he wanted to become a doctor. Indeed, his fascination with medicine stemmed from his passion for experimenting. At the time, he was toying with either becoming a cardiothoracic surgeon or just a chemist since he had a passion for mixing and experimenting.

Regarding advice to other students, he explained that his preparation process for examinations was quite simple – he listened keenly in the class for key points, then he reviewed his notes regularly. He would also try to help his friends with their work, since that re-enforced what he knew.

# GAYROL TAYLOR

Gayrol Taylor, past student of Glenmuir High School, made his mother and teachers proud when he was ranked number four in the world for the 2004 geometrical and mechanical drawing, Cambridge Advanced Level examinations. The unassuming young man who is a devout Christian said that the secret to his success was a combination of 'prayer, studying daily, not allowing the work to pile up and having a good Christian social life.' He was also involved in the Inter-School Christian Fellowship and environmental club while at high school.

The young man from the parish of Clarendon had this piece of advice for fellow students: 'organize yourselves towards studying and don't wait until the last minute. Ask questions and challenge the mind if needs be'.

Gayrol who became a student at the University of Technology, received a three-year scholarship from JAMALCO and was a recipient of the prestigious Gleaner 2004 Honour Award.

# MICHAEL BENT

Michael Bent who went to the Copeland School in London did five advanced level subjects including Mathematics and secured all with distinctions. He was rated amongst the best performers in England in those examinations and was offered an unconditional place at the prestigious Oxford University. However, Bent was unable to take up the offer because he could not pay the fees. Undaunted, he went out and worked as a waiter, tutored students for a year and succeeded in saving enough to get into Oxford.

After completing his first degree Bent enrolled for a Masters degree in Material Science. He said at the time: 'Life here is definitely a learning experience; you meet people from different cultures and background blending to achieve their academic goals.' He went on to lament about the few Black people who were visible at Oxford. He expressed very strong views that there is a need for more Black people and particularly Jamaicans to take up the challenge of attending Oxford University.

For those who wanted to take up the challenge his advice was, 'You must be adjustable, flexible, as there are quite a few things to learn as it is a massive change from being in London or Jamaica.'

# JODI-ANN MAXWELL

Jodi-Ann Maxwell, seventh grader from Ardenne High School, trained by Revd Glen Archer, won the 71st Annual Scripps Howard National Spelling Bee in the USA, in May 1998. The twelve year-old became the champion when she correctly spelled chiaroscurist, which is an artist who uses light and shade to produce the illusion of depth.

Maxwell beat out 248 other contestants aged 9 to 15 from the United States, Guam, Mexico, the U.S. Virgin Islands, the Bahamas and American Samoa. It was Jodi-Ann's first attempt as a national contestant, and she was the first winner from outside the United States. To win, she eliminated Prem Murthy Trivedi, 12, who made his fourth and final appearance in the national spelling bee. As he did in 1997, he finished second. The eighth grader at Lakewood Preparatory School in Howell, New Jersey, was felled by prairillon, which means a small prairie or meadow.

Jodi-Ann's teacher, Revd Glen Archer, said Maxwell trained intensely for eight months before the bee. Maxwell said the toughest part of the bee was the first word because it was the ice-breaker. After that, her nerves calmed down. They had some drama towards the end when a 9 year-old newcomer, Allyson Lieberman, was returned to the competition after the staff discovered she hadn't misspelled her word, 'rescission,' after all. Asked for advice to other students, Maxwell said, 'Trust God, work hard and never lose sight of your goal.'

Maxwell said she wants to be a lawyer because she likes 'to defend people, to push forth their rights.' As the spelling champion, she won US$10,000 in cash and a trophy. On January 11, 2005, Jodi-Ann Maxwell received US$13,000 as the first tranche of a US$30,000 scholarship granted to her by the Caribbean Hotel Foundation. The first year law student [at the time] was extremely happy.

# O'Neil Simpson

Jamaican-born O'Neil Simpson led the team for the Caribbean at the world public speaking competition which took place at the Cave Hill campus of the University of the West Indies in January 2006. There were 53 countries, 148 universities and 324 teams that participated in the world universities debating championships.

Simpson took the World Public Speaking title when he stole the show against teams such as Yale, Harvard, York, and Oxford, with his superior public speaking skills. Leary McLean, the coach and academic advisor said: 'The most revealing aspect of the competition, in my view, was the confirmation that the young people in the Caribbean can stand shoulder to shoulder with anyone else in the world. Cave Hill scored the highest in speaker points and also the crowning glory of it all was the performance of O'Neil Simpson in the finals of the World Public Speaking Competition. People came to the finals to hear O'Neil, he just had the place to himself.'

Simpson said: 'I am apparently now supposed to be a person who can coin words and phrases very well, but for the first time in my life I am absolutely dumbstruck because I did not anticipate the level of experience and success that have metamorphosed themselves into what became the Cave Hill experience at the Worlds 2006.'

Prior to this achievement, the team had won the inter-campus debating trophy back-to-back and won the intercollegiate as well.

# HUGH SMALL

The City and Guilds of London is the UK's most prestigious awarding body and a world leader in international vocational education, providing qualification since 1878, and awarding over one million certificates annually in over 80 countries worldwide. Each year, City and Guilds presents one gold medal for the top student worldwide in each subject. In 2004, two years after been made redundant, Jamaican born Hugh Henry Small was awarded the gold medal for excellence in construction technology. He was the most outstanding student throughout the world who sat the examination.

At age 28, after been made redundant by the public works department, Mr. Small decided to do something with his life. He enrolled on the two-year diploma course in construction at the Brown's Town Community College in St Ann.

He started out by establishing a programme of excellence for his accomplishments in internal examinations. He received the Technical Campus award, Brown's Town Community College Award and the George Thomson award.

The modest scholar did not take the credit all for himself. He said: 'It has been hard work. I have always tried to push my colleagues to work harder because I had seen the potential in others there also. I even encourage them to form a study group.' The study group worked out quite well according to Small, as not only was he able to impart knowledge to his fellow students but he learnt something from them also.

# SEKAYI CAMPBELL

What is exceptionally special about this Jamaican-born graduate of Immaculate Conception High School, is her scholastic achievements the latest of which was that of being the youngest female in the Caribbean to become fellow of the US-based Society of Actuaries in 2004.

Sekayi Campbell had a talk with her father at age eight and that changed her life. She went to her father, Hugh Campbell, one evening very frustrated with an arithmetic problem. Sekayi told him she did not like mathematics. He sat her down and explained that sometimes people develop blocks because of what others say and that although she was a girl she could do math just as well as any boy or even better.

Sekayi maintained very high grades in mathematics throughout her high school and college years. Her hard work and dedication continued at the University of the West Indies where she was awarded first class honours in actuarial science in 1998.

Along the way to the degree, she continued her academic prowess with the Jamaica Adult Suffrage Scholarship to UWI for "A" Level distinction in mathematics, further maths and physics in 1995. She conquered UWI by remaining on the dean's list for the three years at that institution while securing the Merville Campbell prize for lower and upper level mathematics in 1996 and 1997 respectively.

In 1999 she received an Organization of American States (OAS) fellowship and completed a master of mathematics degree in 10 months at the University of Waterloo, Ontario, Canada.

# DR SALEEM JOSEPHS

In May 2006 Saleem Josephs graduated from Columbia University's prestigious school of dental medicine and oral surgery in Manhattan where he was cited as the first student in the world to complete three graduate degrees, including a doctorate, in just five years of study. Saleem was able to not just graduate from all three schools at once but at the top of the class in all three.

Earlier, faculty members at the university had advised Saleem against attempting the 'incredibly difficult' task of combining the school's two dual degree options. He needed at least five years to do the doctorate in dental surgery (DDS) with a master's in business administration (MBA), they told him. So, trying to complete that and the course requirements for a second option – the DDS with a master's in public health (MPH) – in less than six years was inviting failure.

However, Josephs felt doing all three degree programmes simultaneously was a 'unique opportunity' and achievable if he had the right level of discipline, preservation and focus from the very start. Josephs refused to detach himself so he continued to see dental patients and taking public health classes at the same time. It meant that while other business students were carrying a full study load of 15 credits he was taking as many as 21. At that pace, he actually completed the master's degree a year ahead of schedule.

Saleem had moved to Florida in 1996, shortly after graduating from Campion College in Kingston. He attended Ben Lippen High School for two years before going on to major in chemistry at Florida Southern College (FSC). He lost his mother two weeks before his second year at FSC but continued his schooling while grieving and mourning. He admitted that it was his spiritual worldview and his faith in God that helped to stabilize him.

His extraordinary self-motivation may also have been shaped from insights he gained on a visit to Lebanon, shortly after his FSC graduation in 2002. In that year, he toured sections of the Middle East on a self–funded mission.

While in Lebanon, he volunteered at the Al-Amal institute for the disabled and blended easily into the community. What he learnt there taught him to take nothing for granted. At least half the population had applied to migrate to Europe, Canada or North America to search for a better life.

The despair and hopelessness he saw there made him affirm to himself that his story was much more than pursuing three degrees. His story was about seizing and maximizing every opportunity the US had to offer.

# PROFESSOR THE HONOURABLE REX NETTLEFORD

Professor the Honourable Ralston Milton Nettleford was a recipient of the 1957 Rhodes Scholarship and returned to Jamaica in the early 1960s to take up a position at the University of the West Indies. At the UWI he first came to attention as a co-author with M. G. Smith and Roy Augier of a groundbreaking study of the Rastafari movement in 1961. In 1963 he founded the National Dance Theatre Company of Jamaica, an ensemble which under his direction did much to incorporate traditional Jamaican music and dance into a formal ballet-type repertoire.

Beginning with the collection of essays *Mirror, Mirror Jamaica*, in 1971, Nettleford established himself as a serious public historian and social critic. In 1968, Rex Nettleford took over direction of the School for Continuing Studies at the UWI. In 1996, he became Vice-Chancellor of the UWI holding that office until 2004.

Nettleford is a member of the international Committee on Culture, founding Governor of the Canada-based International Development Research Centre, and had acted as expert/consultant to the government of Ghana, FESTAC, CARIFESTA and UNESCO. Professor Nettleford has worked in radio and television as a commentator and has lectured in many countries including India, the Phillipines and Israel.

He has received several awards during the course of his career. In 1975, he received the National Honour of Order of Merit (O.M.), the Gold Musgrave Medal from the Institute of Jamaica and the Living Legend Award from the Black Arts Festival in Atlanta, USA. In 1994, he received the Zora Neale Hurston-Paul Robeson Award for Outstanding Scholarly Achievement from the National Council for Black Studies, USA.

In 2006 he was named chairman of the scientific committee the Slave Route project, by UNESCO.

Sadly, Prof Nettleford passed away after a brief illness on February 3, 2010 having just completed work on *Dance Jamaica: Renewal and Continuty - The NDTC 1962-2008.*

# THAVIA ROBINSON

Robinson's mantra is that living in an inner city community does not determine who you are or who you can become. She was born and raised in Jones Town, beat the odds and became a Rotary World Peace Scholar for the Caribbean and secured two Masters degrees. Although she is presently the co–host of the 'Corner,' a new Talk programme, on News Talk 93 FM, she is planning to complete her doctorate in criminology.

She is the sixth of Pastor Shirley Williams' eight children who is constantly motivated by memories of the tough times in Jones Town. However, the love and support of her mother, who raised her children single–handedly, gave her the strength to succeed.

Robinson attended Wolmers High School for Girls, where she developed a passion for knowledge. Years later, she enrolled at UWI, Mona, where she decided to pursue a difficult double major – International Relations and Political Science.

Later on, she completed a nine–month Masters programme in International Studies, with a focus on geo–narcotics and transnational threats at the University of Bradford in England. Between 2004 and 2005, she did another Masters at Bradford, this time examining the security of small states and counter societies. Both degrees were completed through the Rotary World Peace scholarship.

Her academic performance at Bradford was so impressive that she was honoured with the Most Outstanding International Student Award for her thesis and was also named the most Outstanding Student Overall.

# DR KINGSLEY STEWART

Dr Stewart's story is the exemplification of the dictum: *how far you reach in life is never determined by where you start but where you want to go.* He will admit to you that by age 17 he knew the insides of several police stations yet he went on to graduate with a PhD in Anthropology.

His mother did her best but her best could not care for him and his sister and the father was never around. He could not bear the hunger or that of his sister and he saw how well the street boys were doing so he decided to join them. Later, the courts decided that his mother was not able to control him so he was sent to the Musgrave Boys Home, Homestead Place of Safety and on to the Olivia Boys Home.

Despite the troubles he got into, Kingsley kept going to school and eventually graduated from Calabar High School at age 15. His mother died shortly after from cancer. He was declared an orphan and sent to the Stony Hill Heart Academy.

It was not long after that he got into trouble again. Then something significant happened and led to a change in his life. Well-known attorney-at-law, Hillary Phillips, got him out of trouble for free and told him she did it because he had ability and could do something better with his life. On his release, he was sent through the Jamaica Organization for Youths and Student Travel (JOYST) to Connecticut in the US to a summer counselling camp programme. While at the camp and in speaking to other youths he realized that going on to college was an automatic thing. He also noticed that none of them was any smarter than he was. He realized then that he could go to college too.

The very next semester he was enrolled in North Western Connecticut Community College and also studied for the SAT exams then got accepted to several universities. He took a full scholarship to Vassar College in New York.

In 1993, Stewart graduated with a double degree in African Studies and Psychology. Soon after, he went on the doctoral programme. While at the University of Connecticut he designed and operated a reggae/dancehall show and assumed the stage name 'Ragashanti'. In May 2001 he graduated with a PhD in Anthropology. Stewart is presently a lecturer at the UWI as well as hosting radio show on News Talk 93 FM.

# HECTOR JOSEPHS

Hector Josephs was born in St Andrew in the late nineteenth century. He stood out very early as a bright boy at school so his father decided to get him into one of the best schools in order to further develop the boy's acumen. After the investigation, York Castle High in St Ann was settled on.

At age 19 he came top in the island in the overseas examination and won the Jamaica Scholarship. At the time, a lot of persons could not believe that the grandson of a slave could be so bright. Since there were no universities in Jamaica, he had to go to Cambridge in England in order to take up the scholarship.

In his first year at Cambridge, he came first in his studies. Everybody in Jamaica was proud that a Jamaican had beaten the brightest boys in England. He confirmed his prowess later on when in 1896 he came first in the law examination. Not only did he come first at Cambridge but he was first out of all the students from all over the world.

Josephs returned to Jamaica after university and worked with the government as a lawyer. At age 40, he was made a King's Counsel. As such, he was amongst the first set of Jamaicans to be so honoured.

A turning point came in his life in 1924 when he was appointed Attorney General for the then British Guiana (Guyana). A lot of persons did not believe he was capable because before that only Englishmen were given that job. However, because of his solutions, he soon became extremely popular in British Guiana. After a number of years, he returned to Jamaica where he lived until he died in 1936.

# DR KARL BENNETT

Dr Karl Bennett was born in Jamaica but migrated to Canada in 1959. He took advantage of the education opportunities in Canada by pursuing undergraduate studies at Queen's University then postgraduate studies at McGill University. Since 1966 he has been teaching at the University of Waterloo where he is presently an Associate Professor in the Department of Economics.

His areas of specialization are Economic Development/Trade Policy; Regional Economic Associations; Trade Policy in the Caribbean; the Informal Sector, Economic Development; Exchange Rate Systems, Capital Flights; Monetary Integration.

He has many outstanding achievements and included among them are: UN Consultant in the Caribbean, based in Trinidad; Chair, Department of Economics, 1981–87; taught in the Consortium Graduate School, UWI, Jamaica, 1992; member of the Ontario Premier's Council on Economics Renewal. Since 1979, he has been a Research Associate with the Caribbean Centre for Monetary Studies, formerly the Regional Programme of Monetary Studies. Dr Bennett has also written many monographs, chapters in books, and articles which appear in Social and Economic Studies; Journal of International Development.

# THE LITERARY AND CREATIVE ARTS

# LENNY HENRY – COMEDIAN/ACTOR

Lenworth George Henry was born to Jamaican parents in Dudley, West Midlands in 1958. From a young age in school Lenny read more funny comics, including 'Ironman' than his school books, except English Literature. He did well in literature and got his best Ordinary level grade in it. He made a name for himself at school by doing impersonation of his teachers.

At age 17 in 1975 he won a place on the TV talent show 'New Faces', after doing a Frank Spencer impersonation. Lenny won New Faces and was made several offers. He took up the 'Fosters' and 'Tiswas' later on in 1975. He did a stint with the Black and White Minstrel Show which toured the UK. After five years he left to star and write alongside Tracey Ulman in 'Three of a Kind'. It was here that Lenny met TV producer Paul Jackson who introduced him to the Comic Strip Team.

He hosted 'Saturday Night Live' in 1985 which starred his spouse Dawn French, Rick Mayall and others. In the same year he performed at the Edinburgh Festival and starred in the second series of 'The Lenny Henry Show'. His impersonation of Steve Martin so impressed the people at Disney in the USA that he was offered a three film deal which started with 'True Identity'. It did not make it at the box office and the contract was later cancelled.

Lenny gives back to his community by helping young, Black comedians start their careers. He created the series 'Chef' and encouraged the producers to hire more Black workers on the set. He won a Royal television Society Silver Award medal for outstanding contributions to multi-ethnic programming in the UK, through his production company Crucial Films.

# CLAUDE MCKAY - POET

He was a founding spirit of Harlem Renaissance that burst magnificently upon the literary scene in the 1920s. One of his poems 'If we must Die' was frequently quoted by Winston Churchill in his exhortation to the British people in 1940. The first lines read as follows:

*If we must die, let it not be like hogs hunted and penned in an*
*inglorious spot while round us bark the mad and hungery dogs,*
*making the mark at our accursed lot.*

Born September 15, 1889 in Sunnyville Clarendon, McKay was the youngest of eleven children of Thomas McKay and Hannah Ann Edwards. At age seven, he went to live with his older brother, Uriah, an elementary school teacher near Montego Bay. By age 10, he was writing sophisticated poetry, and reading every book he could find.

Later, McKay dabbled with cabinet-making and served a short while in the Jamaica Constabulary Force whilst in Spanish Town before leaving Jamaica in 1912 to attend the Tuskagee Institute in Alabama where he hoped to study Agronomy. In 1912 at the age of 23, he wrote two volumes of dialect poetry, Songs of Jamaica and Constab Ballads. For a while he resided in Harlem where he authored a book entitled *Home to Harlem*, which achieved bestseller status.

Long before he wrote his last book *Harlem Glory*, he was recognized for his unique and distinct Jamaican poetry, his rebel pioneering in the Harlem literary upsurge of the 1920s, and his influence on the rise of the Negritude movement of Africa and Europe.

He never became a scientist and he never returned to Jamaica before he died in Chicago in 1948, but in his heart and in his poetry he never really left. He would travel all over the world – to London, Moscow, Paris, Marseilles, as well as Morocco. Wherever he went, he would write about Jamaica. Indeed, in a lifetime of 58 years he had written 17 books, seven of which were published posthumously.

# Roger R. Cross – Film

Roger Cross, born in Christiana Jamaica, became a contemporary actor and has made numerous appearances in several movies and television series, mostly on productions done in Canada.

His mother worked at Grand Cayman airport before migrating with the family to Vancouver, Canada when Roger Cross was 11. On the flight to Canada, the captain allowed him to visit the cockpit. It was then that he made up his mind that he wanted to fly airplanes.

He graduated from Trinity Western University with a Bachelor's Degree in Aviation and General Studies with the firm intention to become a pilot. However, fate had other things in mind for Cross. The stock market crash in 1987 resulted in a lack of jobs for young pilots. He did a stint in charter flying and while waiting for a flying job he became an occasional film stuntman.

Cross had acted in several church plays, and although he enjoyed them he had never considered acting as a career. However, after doing a lot of stunts he enrolled in the Break Academy and studied acting.

His big break came when a friend introduced him to an acting coach who was casting for *The International Rescue*, a WWII movie. Cross read for a role and got the part. The movie was filmed in China, Vietnam and Burma.

Cross was cast in guest roles on such hit TV series as *The X-Files*, *Sliders*, *Stargate SG-1*, *Highlander: The Series*, *Relic Hunter*, *The 4400*, *Higher Ground* and *Star Trek: Enterprise*. He was also a regular on the sci-fi series First Wave and appeared in such films as *The Chronicles of Riddick*, *X2*, *Ballistic: Ecks vs. Sever*, and *Beautiful Joe*. His most recent role has been Agent Curtis Manning on *24*. His role began at the start of the show's fourth season in 2005 as a recurring character; however, he later became a main cast member.

Cross can be seen in the Oliver Stone film, *World Trade Center*, which was released in August 2006. Cross also plays the character of Barry in the 2008 movie *Mad Money*. He currently resides in Los Angeles and has one son.

# MICHAEL CHAMBERS – ARTIST

Michael migrated from Jamaica to Canada in 1972 and because of his sheer hard work was later described as 'the quintessential Canadian Artist' for his challenging photographic work. In the early 1990s, he was a contributing photographer to *Now* and *Word* magazines. In 1995, his image, *The Watermelon* became one of the most controversial in contemporary art. In 1998, he presented a ten-year, retrospective at the Thames Art Gallery at Chatham, Ontario. 'Spectators are no More' were also presented to rave reviews.

Chambers has exhibited internationally in the US, Japan, South Africa, the UK and the Caribbean. In addition to his works for galleries and museums, he has collaborated on films including: 'Journey to Justice'; 'Esther, Baby and Me'; 'Raising Cain'; and 'The Gospel According to Mary'. Chambers was also the subject of the NFB documentary, 'The Photographer: An Artist's Journey'. He is the subject of the jazz recording, 'Michael the Photographer', by Neil Braithwaite and David Williams.

Chambers has been interviewed and profiled in the media including television and print, and his work appears in national and international publications. He was also the creative Director of *Deagon* magazine; has produced three AIDS awareness posters for the AIDS Committee of Toronto; and has lectured across Ontario since 1993.

He has been honoured with the Mosaic Award in 2000; reviewed in: *Revue Noire*; *British Journal of Photography*; *Elle*; *Mix Magazine*; *Soul*; *Venus*; *Gleaner*; *PhotoDigest*; *Toronto Life* and *Toronto Star*.

# Linton Kwesi Johnson – Poet

Linton Kwesi Johnson was born in Chapelton, Clarendon, Jamaica. He migrated to England in 1963 and went to Tulse Hill Secondary School, then studied Sociology at Goldsmiths College, University of London. Today, Linton is known as the world's first dub poet.

At school, he joined the Black Panthers, organised a poetry workshop within the organisation and developed his work with Rasta Love, a group of poets and drummers. In 1977 he was awarded a C. Day Lewis Fellowship, becoming the writer-in-residence for the Borough of Lambeth in London for that year. Later, he worked as the Library Resources and Education Officer at the Kiskidee Centre, the first home for Black Theatre Art.

In 1974, his first collection of poetry, *Voices of the Living and the Dead*, was published in 'Race Today'. *Dread Beat an' Blood*, his second collection, was published in 1975 by Bogle L'Overture and was also the title of his first LP, released by Virgin in 1978. In the same year, the documentary film 'Dread Beat an' Blood', was released. It was a documentary on Johnson's work. In 1980, 'Race Today' published his third book, *Inglan is a Bitch*.

Linton Kwesi Johnson was made an Associate Fellow of Warwick University and Honorary Fellow of Wolverhampton Polytechnic. He is the only living poet to be published by 'Penguin Classics'.

# Neville Clarke – Artist

Neville migrated to Canada in 1974 and was well known there for his portraits and his work in watercolours. His paintings are said to 'reflect the current social and economic situation'. For Neville, the figure is the medium through which he communicates and expresses sympathy, hope and human dignity. Through his paintings, Neville Clarke explores the issues of Black identity, hopes to re-educate Canadian society, and aims to influence and encourage Black creativity.

Neville lectures and make presentations on Canadian Art at a number of locations including the Varley Gallery in Unionville and the Robert McLaughlin Gallery. He is a member of several organizations including the Society of Canadian Artists; the Ontario Society of Artists; the Canadian Institute of Portrait Artists; founder, Society of African–Canadian Artists. Since 2001 he has been the President of the Canadian Society of Painters in Watercolour, the first person of African descent to hold this position.

Honours he has received include: One of his paintings has been included in the Prince of Wales Collection, UK, 2001; Outstanding Established Artist Award; Charles Comfort Medal; the A.J. Casson Medal twice, 1995 and 1999. His work has also been reviewed in *A Dictionary of Canadian Artists* and Exhibition Catalogues.

# JOEL AUGUSTUS ROGERS – WRITER/HISTORIAN

Joel Rogers was to a great extent a self-trained man. However, some of the most eminent scholars of the twentieth century have acknowledged their debt to him. William E.B. DuBois, said of him: 'no man living has revealed so many important facts about the African race as Rogers'.

Rogers was a field anthropologist whose travels took him to over sixty different countries researching and observing. Born in Negril, Jamaica in 1883 to local school teachers, he went to the US, settling in Chicago for a while but spending most of his life in Harlem, New York. He had been told when he was a child in Sunday School that God had cursed the Black man and made him inferior. He wanted to prove otherwise.

He went all over the globe like a detective and carried out exhaustive primary research into the global history of African people. For fifty years of his life, he investigated and reported the accomplishments of ancient and contemporary African people and their place in history, contributing to such publications as *The Crisis, American Mercury*, *The Messenger*, *The Negro World* and *Survey Graphic.* He contributed a feature to the *Pittsburg Courier* entitled 'Your History'.

1930 was a high point in Rogers' career. In that year, he went to Ethiopia as a correspondent for the *New York Amsterdam News* to attend the coronation of Emperor Haile Selassie I, who presented him with the Coronation Medal. In the same year, he spoke at the International Congress of Anthropology held in Paris.

His organizational membership included the Paris Society of Anthropology, the American Geographical Society, the American Association for the Advancement of Science and the Academy of Political Science.

When several publishing houses refused to publish his material, he never gave up; he published them himself. He wrote and published 16 different books and pamphlets. His work covered the entire spectrum of the global African community, from ancient and modern Africa to Asia, Australia, the South Pacific, Europe and the Western Hemisphere.

# ANDREA LEVY - AUTHOR

In 1948 the father of Andrea Levy was one of the Jamaican pioneers who sailed on the *Windrush* to England, seeking a better life. Andrea grew up in one of the Black communities in England, an experience that moulded her unusual perspective of the country of her birth – neither feeling totally part of the society nor a total outsider.

Andrea did not start writing until she was in her mid 30s. At that time there was little written about the Black British experience in England. After attending writing workshops Levy began to write the novels that she, as a young woman, had always wanted to read. In her first three novels she explored, from different perspectives, the problems faced by Black British-born children of Jamaican emigrants.

In her first novel, the semi-autobiographical *Every Light in the House Burnin* (1994), the story is of a Jamaican family living in London in the 1960s. *Never Far from Nowhere* (1996), her second, is set during the 1970s and tells the story of two very different sisters living in a London council estate. In *Fruit of Lemon* (1999), Faith Jackson, a young Black woman, visits Jamaica after suffering a nervous breakdown and discovers a previously unknown personal history.

In her most celebrated novel, *Small Island*, she examines the experiences of those of her father's generation who returned to Britain after being in the Royal Air Force (RAF) during the Second World War. But more than just the story of the Jamaicans who came looking for a new life in the mother country, she uses her understanding of the white society to show the adjustments and the problems faced by the English people whom those Jamaicans came to live amongst.

Immigration changes everyone's lives and in *Small Island*. Levy examines not only the conflicts of two cultures thrown together after a terrible war, but also the kindness and strength people can show to each other. For Andrea Levy, acknowledging the role played by all sides in this change is an important part of understanding the process so all can go on to create a better future together.

Andrea Levy has been the recipient of an Arts Council Award and her second novel, *Never Far from Nowhere*, was long listed for the Orange Prize. *Small Island*, her most recent novel, is the winner of the Orange Prize for Fiction, The Whitbread Novel award and the Commonwealth Writer's Prize. She has also written short stories that have been read on radio and published in newspapers.

# UNA MARSON - WRITER/BROADCASTER

Una Marson was born in 1905 at the Baptist Manse in Santa Cruz to parents Revd Marson and his wife, Ada. At school she demonstrated her academic prowess by coming first in the primary school examinations in the parish of St Elizabeth. Una was indeed very bright and did very well at the Hampton High School.

When she left school, she was hailed as one of the fastest typists in Jamaica. She secured employment with ease as a result. Although she excelled in writing short stories and poems she never got the credit she was due because she was a woman. She went to Kingston in 1928 and organized women office workers into groups calling for better pay and conditions.

Una continued writing then started a magazine in which she portrayed Jamaican culture and published her stories and poems about Jamaican life. She even wrote a play, 'pocomania', which was modestly successful. Una decided she wanted to learn more about the wider world, and she left Jamaica for England in 1932.

In London Una was snapped up by the British Broadcasting Corporation (BBC) then one of the first radio stations with millions of listeners worldwide. Una Marson was one of the first female voices to be heard on such broadcasts.

She was in London when the Italian army attacked Ethiopia, an event that was to spark her interest in politics. Emperor Haile Selassie had to leave Ethiopia and sought refuge in London where Una Marson met and worked with him as his secretary in his efforts to regain his throne. Most of his speeches were written by her. When the Americans and the British won the war in 1945, the Italians had to leave Ethiopia. The Emperor reclaimed his throne and said publicly that he could not have succeeded without the help of Una Marson.

# CHRIS BROWNE - WRITER

On May 18, 2006 at the Cannes Film Festival in France, Jamaican Director/Scriptwriter Chris Browne was awarded the prestigious Hartley-Merrill International Scriptwriting Prize for his script, 'Ghett'a Life'. This was the first time anyone from the Caribbean had won this prize in its 16 years of existence and the award's third time to this part of the world.

Securing funding for the film had been extremely challenging for Browne. The idea for the film was born in 2001 when he wrote a treatment/outline for a movie and took it with him to Cannes. He was able to whip up much interest and commitment for some of the funding. The possibility of a US$3 million budget then became real when British producers took interest in the project and were able to engage the British Film Council. Unfortunately, the programme crashed when the British Film Council had personnel changes, bringing funding to a complete halt.

# ZADIE SMITH – AUTHOR

Zadie Smith of Jamaican parentage won the Best Book category for the Eurasia region in the Commonwealth Writers Prize (CWP), the Commonwealth Foundation announced in London in early 2006. Smith, whose mother is Jamaican, won for her third book *On Beauty* which portrays the interaction between two families with different beliefs and looks at the friendship and feuds caused by a gulf in political, ideological and social values.

An international judging panel chaired by Professor Angela Smith, director of the Centre of Commonwealth Studies, University of Stirling, felt that '*On Beauty* was written at such a high level of intelligence and style that it gleams. The people in it seem to have been leading real lives before the reader joins the story. It domesticates fashionable argument and posturing effortlessly, and redefines beauty.'

On learning she had won the competition which included competitors from Europe and South Asia, Smith said she was honoured to be included on a list of such international variety and global reach. 'It makes me feel part of a community of writers and that's a very rewarding sensation,' said Ms. Smith.

Her first novel, *White Teeth*, won the overall Commonwealth Writers Prize for 'best first book' award in 2001.

# Christopher John Farley – Author

Christopher John Farley began his writing career with *Time* magazine as a music writer and worked his way to the top as Senior Editor. Farley, whose grandparents lived in Mocho, Jamaica, wrote the critically acclaimed novel *My Favourite* War set during the Gulf War; a novel about pirate Anne Bonny, *Kingston by Starlight* and recently, *Before the Legend: The Rise of Bob Marley*.

Farley returns regularly to Jamaica to see his brother Jonathan who graduated from both Harvard and Oxford and is currently employed at the University of the West Indies as Head of the Mathematics and Computer Science Department.

Farley believes that *Before the Legend* fills many gaps in Bob Marley's life and was a book that needed to be written. 'There have been plenty a book about Marley, but his real story has not been told. There are many new findings and new stories in the book. For many years, other biographers have written that Marley's father, Norval, was a white British captain. My book shows that Norval Marley was actually discharged as a private, born in Jamaica, and was a person of colour who was accepted as white.'

In writing the book, Farley's respect for Bob Marley and the Wailers increased tremendously. That respect increased when he learnt more about the many obstacles – financial, social, political - that Bob and the band had to overcome.

## Lillian Allen – Author/Writer

Lillian Allen went to Canada in 1969 and grew up to pursue a writing path to success. Today, she is an award-winning and internationally renowned poet and writer of short stories and plays. As one of the pioneers, she has specialized in the writing and performing of dub poetry, a highly politicized form of poetry, which is often set to music.

Her recordings, 'Revolutionary Tea Party' and 'Conditions Critical,' won Juno Awards in 1986 and 1988. Her works appear independently and in anthologies. She has spent almost 20 years writing, publishing, and performing her work in Canada, the US and Europe. Allen has worked in film, both as a featured artist, as a co-director and co-producer. She has worked on films such as 'Revolution from the Beat', 'Unnatural Causes,' 'Rhythm and Hardtimes' and 'Blakk wi Blakk'.

Allen is a leading expert on cultural diversity and culture in Canada and has been a consultant and advisor to all levels of government and to community groups. She has initiated or facilitated the establishment of a number of organizations in the Black community and in various culturally diverse communities. Among her many awards are: Honorary Doctorate, University of Toronto; Margo Binhardt Award – City of Toronto & the Toronto Arts Foundation; Foundation of Canadian Poetry, League of Canadian Poets; Ontario Volunteer Service Award; Outstanding Contribution to the Arts Award.

# LOUISE BENNETT COVERLY – AUTHOR/FOLKLORIST

Louise Bennett Coverly was born and raised in Jamaica then migrated to Canada in 1987. The Hon. Dr Louise Bennett-Coverly, affectionately known by her stage name 'Miss Lou' is Jamaica's foremost and most renowned folklorist, writer and storyteller. Known and admired the world over, she climbed to fame by creating acceptance for the Jamaican dialect and through her artistry – seen in acting, broadcasting, theatre, literature and poetry – elevating it as a legitimate form of speech which is representable of a key component of Jamaican culture.

She began writing and performing dialect verse at age 13, at a time when Standard English was considered the norm and the ideal to which most people aspired. In 1939, she started her acting career while in high school, and was discovered by Eric Coverly, a popular musician who would later become her husband. In 1945, she won a scholarship to the Royal Academy of Dramatic Arts in London. While there and still a student, she hosted the live radio show, 'Caribbean Carnival' on the BBC.

During her second stay in London in 1950, she hosted a second programme for the BBC, 'West Indian Guest Night,' which introduced emerging West Indian talent.

In Jamaica, her verses, written in dialect were published in the country's newspaper *The Daily Gleaner* and also performing them on the stage and on radio along with her prose monologues. She hosted radio shows, 'Laugh with Louise' and 'Miss Louise's Views' which were on the air for 15 years, as well as 'The Lou and Ranny Show' with comedian Ranny Williams.

On stage, she appeared in a number of productions including the annual Jamaican Pantomime. She retired from the stage in 1975 but continued to host a television programme for children, 'Ring Ding' for twelve years. This programme allowed children from all over the country to participate and showcase their talent in the performing arts.

Her film credits include 'Calypso' and 'Club Paradise'. Her song, 'Going Home,' used in the film 'Milk and Honey', was nominated for a Genie award. In 1989, she was appointed Ambassador-At-Large for Culture by the Jamaican government. Over the years Louise Bennett-Coverley has performed and lectured all over the world, promoting Jamaican history and culture and creating awareness and pride amongst Jamaicans for folk stories and songs. Her works are said to, '... ridicule class and colour prejudice, and criticize people ashamed of being Jamaican or ashamed of being black.'

She has received many honours and awards including 'Most Important Theatre Personality of the 20th Century', by the International Theatre Institute; Member of the Order of Merit (OM) for her distinguished contribution to the development of the Arts and Culture; Member of the British Empire (MBE) for work in Jamaican literature and theatre; Norman Manley Award for Excellence; Order of Jamaica for work in the field of Native Culture; Hon D. Litt; York University 1988 and UWI 1982; Gold Musgrave Medal for development of the Arts in Jamaica and the Caribbean.

# DR AFUA COOPER – WRITER

Afua Cooper migrated to Canada in 1980 where she built a reputation as a poet and a historian. She is the author of four books of poetry, and is credited with co-authoring the first book on Black Women's history in Canada, *We are Rooted Here and They Can't Pull Us YP: Essays in African-Canadian Women's History* (1999). She is the first woman in Canada to graduate with a doctorate in African-Canadian History.

Cooper lectures at the Ryerson University and in 2002, curated two exhibitions in Toronto, on Black History and life in nineteenth century Toronto, displayed at Royal Museum and at McKenzie House.

She has received many honours, including: Honorable Colonel for contributions to the study of Kentucky's history and life of Blacks; Fellowship, Brown University; Joseph Brant Award, Best Book on Ontario History; Casa de las Americas prize for poetry.

Her published works include: 'Utterances & Incantations: Women, Poetry, & Dub', (1999); 'Memories Have Tongue'(1992); Articles in: *Atlantis*, a Women's Study Journal*; Canadian review of American Studies and Ontario History; Copper Woman*(2006) and *The Hanging of Angelique* (2006).

# SPORTS

# John Barnes – Sports

John Barnes, son of an army officer in Jamaica, started his career in football at Watford, England in 1981. He later moved to Liverpool where he spent ten years and helped them to win the FA Cup and two league championships. His arrival on the international scene was indelibly, marked by a solo goal against Brazil. He went on to score 12 goals, whilst representing England 78 times.

In the 1997-98 season, he moved to Newcastle United where he made many impressive sorties before ending his Premiership career at Charlton. He later teamed up with his former playing colleague Kenny Dalglish to become head coach at Celtic.

He has been working as a match analyst on ITV's coverage of international and domestic football for several years including working on coverage of the 1998 World Cup in France, Euro 2000 in Holland and Belgium and World Cup 2002 in Korea/Japan.

John Barnes served as an ambassador for Save the Children, with several trips including visits to Kenya and Ethiopia. In the last quarter of 2008, he returned to Jamaica to take up the post of Technical Director of Jamaica's national team, the Reggae Boyz.

# JOEL JACKSON - MOTOR RACING

Karter, Joel Jackson, became the first Jamaican driver to race Formula One when he competed in the Formula BMW series which began May 2006. He had successfully completed training in Spain and test sessions in the US before being signed to race in the season of the Formula BMW US series with the Gelles racing team.

The series is considered an entry-level programme for Formula One drivers and Jackson, who has put his University Career on hold to enter at the highest level was extremely confident about doing well.

Jackson is a past student of Ardenne High School where he graduated in 2005 with nine CXCs and two 'A' Levels. Indeed, he excelled even before that as one of Jamaica's top Karters.

His seven year racing career has seen him win several races and breaking a number of track records. He was the light class champion in 2004 and the Rostax Max Challenge Champion in 2005. The young racer has developed a reputation over the years for taking pole position in most of the events he entered. From a very early age he had a keen interest in motor sports and is a moderator on the popular Wheels Jamaica web-based racing forum. Jackson firmly believes that there is space for more Jamaicans to get involved in international racing.

# MERLENE OTTEY - ATHLETICS

Ottey was born May 10, 1960, at Pondside in Hanover and at the age of 15 started to show that she had better than average skills on the track, in the 100 and 200 meters events. She progressed while she was a student at the Rusea's High School and Vere Technical High School, and by 1979, at age 19 she was ranked number 13 in the world in the 200 Metres, had a best time of 23.10 seconds and won a bronze medal in the 200m and a silver in the 4x100m relay at the Pan American Games.

Merlene represented Jamaica in the Olympic Games for the first time in 1980 in Monaco and won a bronze medal in the 200m event. That year she dominated the competition in the indoor and college meets running for the University of Nebraska, from which she graduated in 1983 with a B.A degree. In 1980 she was ranked third in the world over 200m. At the Olympics in Los Angeles in 1984 she won bronze medals in both the 100m and 200m events.

In 1995 Ottey set a new World indoor record for the 50m event and in 1996 she won silver medals in the 100m and 200m events at the Atlanta Olympic Games. When Ottey won silver relay medal at the 2000 Sydney Olympic Games, this gave her eight Olympic medals, the most by any woman in the sport.

Overall, she has won 14 medals at the world championships in individual and relay events and is the only athlete who won an Olympic event at age 20 and again at age 40. Indeed, at onc time Ottey ranked in the top ten in the world in 200m for a record 12 consecutive years and won the 'Sportswoman of the Year' award in Jamaica on 13 occasions.

# VERONICA CAMPBELL - ATHLETICS

Veronica Campbell was born to Cecil Campbell and Pamela Bailey in Trelawny, Jamaica on May 15th 1982. Campbell has nine brothers and sisters. She attended Clarendon High School before pursuing higher education in the United States. In the United States, Campbell attended Barton County Community College in Great Bend, Kansas. There, she set several records and won many titles including four national titles in the 60m, 100m and 200m dashes indoors and outdoors. She set the current record for Barton County in the outdoor 100m and 200m dashes.

Campbell also excelled in academics earning an Associates Degree from Barton County in 2002 with a grade point average of 3.8. She went on to attend the University of Arkansas. Inspired to compete in Track and Field by fellow Jamaican athletes Donald Quarrie and Merlene Ottey, Campbell began competing internationally. She won the 100m at the 1999 World Youth Championships. In 2000, Campbell also competed in the Olympics earning a Silver medal on the team that finished 2nd to the Bahamas. She found herself running with her idol, Merlene Ottey, on the team.

In 2004, Campbell came in first in the 200m in the Grand Prix at Linz, Austria. Later that year, she would make history as the first woman from Jamaica or the Caribbean to win an Olympic Gold medal in a sprint race-women's 200m at the 2004 Olympic Games in Athens, Greece. On Wednesday August 25th 2004 Campbell ran her personal best of 22.05 in the 200M beating Allyson Felix to the finish line earning Jamaica's 6th Gold Medal in Olympic History. Campbell would go on to win another Gold in the women's 4x100m relay and Bronze in the women's 100m.

At the World Games 2007, she won the women's 100m and earned a Silver Medal in the 200m. She intends to pursue a career in business or as a teacher.

# ASAFA POWELL – ATHLETICS

Asafa Powell is from a strong Christian background. Powell, one of six boys born to Keith and Cislyn Powell in St Catherine, Jamaica became a Christian at age 12 and grew up with great respect for his parents who are strict disciplinarians.

Asafa was so disciplined that if he was on the outside of the property and he heard the sound of his father's car approaching he would run straight inside and settle down before his dad came inside. His mother thought that is how he started practicing for Track.

At the Olympic games in Athens 2004, everyone expected Powell to get a medal but that did not happen. However, at the Athens Super Grand Prix Meet a few weeks later, he rebounded. He demonstrated remarkable resilience by winning the 100m in a new-world record time of 9.77. Powell, later, equaled it twice.

In August 2007, at the World Games in Osaka, Japan, the world expected Asafa to win gold but disappointment struck again, he earned a bronze. Powell showed his resilience again by lowering the world record to 9.74 within a few weeks. Powell holds the record of being the athlete who has recorded more sub-10.00 seconds in the 100m than any other athlete.

# USAIN BOLT - ATHLETICS

His name and achievements in athletics have earned him the media nickname 'Lightning Bolt'. Usain Bolt is the only junior to have run the 200m under 20 seconds. As holder of the world junior and Jamaican national records, Bolt started running while in primary school. After competing for his parish of Trelawny at the annual national primary schools meeting, his coach convinced him to pursue track and field and that year he entered William Knibb High School where he pursued Track.

It was not until his third year at High School, in 2001, that Bolt won his first medal at the annual High School Championships, finishing second in 22.04 in the 200m. At age 15, he took the 200/400 double at the High School Championships, Carifta and the CAC Junior Championships, laying the foundation for a big run at the World Junior Championships in his home country, in Kingston.

Bolt's record runs continued in 2004. He had turned professional and lowered the world junior 200m record of 20.13 seconds he shared with American Roy Martin, as he became the first junior athlete to break 20 seconds, with his Carifta Games winning time of 19.93 in Bermuda.

Unfortunately, leg ailments put paid to the Olympic medal winning promise offered by the record run and Bolt was eliminated in the first round of the 200m at the Olympic Games in Athens in 2004. Bolt has since broken 20 seconds on five occasions. That includes his national senior record of 19.75 at the 2007 Jamaican National Championships, breaking the 36-year-old record of his hero, Don Quarrie, by 0.11.

On May 3, 2008, Bolt ran 9.76 in the 100m at the Jamaican Invitational, then the second fastest legal performance in the history of the event, behind colleague Asafa Powell. Later that month, on 31 May 2008, Bolt ran 9.72, establishing a new world record in the 100m at the Reebok Grand Prix in New York, breaking the 9.74-second record of Asafa Powell. This was only his 5th senior run over the distance.

He became the first man, in 2008 to set three world records in 100m, 200m and 4 x 100m relay at a single Olympics. Then, in 2009, he became the first man to hold the 100m and 200m World and Olympics titles at the same time. The records are 9.58s for the 100m and 19.19s for the 200m. Bolt's career to date is recorded in his autobiography published in the Caribbean in 2010 by Ian Randle Publishers.

# STEVE BUCKNOR – CRICKET

In 2005, umpire, Steve Bucknor made cricketing history when he officiated in the second test between fierce rivals India and Pakistan in Calcutta, March 16-20. It was his 100th test match. As such, he had created an almost unassailable world record for the most appearances in test matches as an umpire.

The Montegonian first equaled, then broke the legendary 'Dickie' Bird's record of 66 tests in 2002 in a series between Pakistan and New Zealand and has since gone on to establish himself as one of the best in the game.

Bucknor, who was the first person to be a FIFA referee and test umpire, said while it was good to achieve a milestone that was not his intention.

Bucknor who also led his alma mater Cornwall College to several schoolboy titles in the mid-1980s, made his debut in the fourth test between the West Indies and India in Kingston, Jamaica in April 1989 and has since then also umpired in 131 one day internationals (ODI). His total is the third highest number of ODI's with Rudi Koertzen of South Africa and David Shepherd of England having officiated more ODIs.

He became the first recipient of the international cricket club (ICC) Golden Bails award, part of the umpire recognition programme.

# STEPHEN FRANCIS – ATHLETICS

Stephen Francis, is the coach extraordinaire and CEO of the MVP athletics club 'Maximizing Velocity and Power' which has achieved success against the odds. Francis is the coach of Asafa Powell who was at one time the 'world's fastest man'. An unknown in 2002, Powell has improved markedly, moving from personal best of 10.70 in 2001 to 9.74 (world record) in 2007. Asafa went on to be the only man to have run legally under 10.00 seconds twelve times in a single season. Coach Francis is also the coach of Brigitte Foster–Hylton who broke the Commonwealth Games record in 100m hurdles at the Commonwealth Games in 2006 in Melbourne, Australia, and won the World Championships in Berlin in 2009.

Stephen Francis, the son of training consultant Vincent Francis and Nurse Derman Francis, made enormous sacrifices along the way to the achievement of MVP. He could have chosen an easier path. In the early 1990s after years as a high school coach at Wolmers Boys' School where he also taught, Francis went to the University of Michigan to complete an MBA in accounting and management as a springboard into the corporate world. On his return to Jamaica, he joined the international firm KMPG Peat Marwick and did very well until he decided that his heart was really into athletics. He wanted to coach full-time.

Francis had started coaching when, while completing a first degree at the University of the West Indies in 1982, he offered coaching help to his brother Paul Francis with good results. He was never an athlete himself, but he states that he loves sports and that he came by his expertise through reading. He started out at the Mico library and, as his income grew, began purchasing and bringing books into the island on the subject of coaching and improving athletic performance.

It was Brigitte Foster-Hylton's return to Jamaica without a coach that led him to the major transformation. Someone recommended him to her and they were both impressed with each other. However, Francis had fallen on hard times and even had to sell his car but he never gave up. He recruited Asafa Powell in 2001 when no one knew him. Coach Francis enjoys dealing with the underdogs then turns them into world champions. Although facilities at the MVP club at UTECH are not the best in the world the club attracts other stars such as Sherone Simpson, Michael Frater, and sprinters from England and Trinidad.

# Dudley and Chris Stokes – Bobsleighing

As a country in the tropics, no one expected Jamaicans to train and enter events on ice in the Winter Olympics. Yet Dudley and Chris Stokes did that by entering the bobsleigh event and demonstrated the Jamaican brand of audacity by capturing the imagination of the world and won hearts everywhere, inspiring a successful movie, a book and a generation of Jamaicans.

The two boys were born to parents, Rev. Dr Dudley Stokes and Dr Blossom O'Mealy-Nelson. Because of the father's job as a parson, the family was constantly on the move in Jamaica and the Caribbean. Chris later went to college in the US while Dudley joined the army and went to the famous and elite Sandhurst in England for military training.

Dudley returned to Jamaica, well trained and as fit as a fiddle with a lot of time on his hands and not much to do. At the same time William Maloney, an American living in Jamaica decided he wanted to get involved in an Olympic sport. Mike Fennel, head of the Jamaica Olympic Association, advised him to find a sport that Jamaicans did not already do, form a federation, meet the qualifying standards and get acceptance from the sport's governing body.

Maloney had seen Jamaicans in the push kart derby which was similar to the bobsleigh so he decided on bobsleighing. He could not find any recruits so he went to Col. Ken Barnes who was in charge of sports at the Jamaica Defence Force. He wanted a team to enter the Olympics which was three months away. Lt. Dudley Stokes was one of the soldiers chosen.

A team was put together and they went off to training in the US with sub-standard equipment, living a hand-to-mouth existence with all of them sharing the same hotel room. Some days before the start of the events a teammate was injured and Chris Stokes was called to replace him. Chris was being asked to participate in an event which normally took three years of preparation. The rest of the team had three months and he would have three days.

On day two of the events with the fantastic speed of Chris Stokes, their sled achieved the seventh fastest push time and fourth out of over 30 countries. It was sweet revenge on those, including the American journalists, who ridiculed them.

Then, on the same run, the sled careened out of control and ended up in a major crash witnessed by 100 million viewers at Calgary and on television worldwide. Dudley broke his collarbone and Chris dislocated his. Although it was an embarrassment, that crash formed the spectacular climax to the movie 'Cool Runnings' which the team's overall success was to inspire. The lesson for the team was that the big success in life was actually born out of huge failures. In other words, one cannot truly succeed until one has truly failed.

In the 1992 Winter Olympics in France, the team came 24th. The brothers regrouped acquiring the services of Winston Watt and Wayne Thomas who proved to be two of the best pushers in the world. By 1993 they were more than ready for the 1994 Olympics.

It was another eventful time for the team in Lillehammer, Norway. Despite an overweight sled that caused the two-man team to be disqualified, they finished 14th overall but more importantly, beat the mighty US. The actual placing in terms of country was number eight. It shocked the world. Hollywood became interested. Out of that interest came as the feature length movie 'Cool Runnings' which was partially shot on location at Flint River in the parish of Hanover.

# DONOVAN BAILEY – ATHLETICS

Donovan Bailey left Jamaica for Canada at age 12 in 1980. He graduated from college with a Diploma in Business Administration and started his own Telemarketing Company. He started running seriously in 1994. Soon, Donovan became a five-time world and Olympic Champion, and the first man in history to achieve, in a single year, the titles of Olympic Champion, World Champion and World Record Holder. Indeed, *Track and Field News* named him 'Sprinter of the Decade' (1990s) and one of the all-time most dominant sprinters.

Bailey is the winner of several world class sprint competitions, including eight-time Canadian Champion, Pan American Games Champion, Commonwealth Games Champion, World Champion and Olympic Champion, Francophone Games Champion and Goodwill Games Champion.

He still holds the Olympic Record for the 100m and World Record for the 50m. At the 1996 Atlanta Olympic Games, he set a world record of 9.84 seconds in the 100m sprint and led Canada's men's 4x100m relay team to a gold medal victory.

He is the subject of a 1998 documentary, 'Olympic warrior: Donovan Bailey's War'. Since retirement from competitive athletics, he has become involved in several business ventures as well as community efforts including the Canadian Cancer Society, Ontario Lung Association, Big Brothers and Big Sisters. He has also created the Donovan Bailey Foundation, committed to the advancement and financial assistance of Canada's most talented amateur athletes.

The many awards he received include Athlete of the Year; Lou Marsh Trophy and Canadian Leadership Award.

# CHARMAINE CROOKS – ATHLETICS

Charmaine left Jamaica for Canada in 1973 and became a five-time Olympian, representing Canada from 1980-97 in athletics and competing in track events (400m, 800m, and 4x400m relay). She was the opening ceremony Flag Bearer at the 1996 Olympics and won a silver medal in the 1984 Olympics in the 4x400m relay. Her other achievements include being Pan Am World Cup and Commonwealth Games Gold Medallist and 11-times Canadian national champion in 400m and 800m. She is the first Canadian woman to run the 800m under two minutes.

Charmaine was elected as a member of the International Olympic Committee (IOC) in 1996 and 2000, served as a member of the Toronto 2008 Olympic Bid Committee and is a founding member of the independent IOC Ethics Commission and current member of the IOC Press Commission. Charmaine's current activities include:

- President of NGU Consulting which provides strategic counseling for sports organizations and corporations
- Freelance TV host
- Producer and motivational speaker
- Host/Analyst on TV broadcasts of Canadian national games
- Creator and producer of the comic relief style show 'No laughing Matter' which raises funds for cancer research
- Creator of 'Sports Cares' which helps disadvantaged youths to get involved in sports and healthy lifestyles.

Charmaine has received several honours including being inducted into Athletics Hall of Fame, University of Texas, 2001; Bruce Kidd Award for Athletic Leadership; Governor General's Award for Community Service and the John F. Bassett Award for outstanding community work and sporting excellence.

# Fashion Design and Modelling

# JESSICA OGDEN - DRESS DESIGNER

Jessica was born and raised in Jamaica. Later, she attended the Rhode Island School of Design in the US and graduated from the Byam Shaw School of Art in London. Her career in clothing started in 1992 as a volunteer for Oxfam's 'NoLoGo', the eco-friendly design collective whose ethos was to re-use pieces found in charity stores by turning them into new garments.

Jessica's fascination with old and distressed fabrics has been a continuing theme in all the collections since the launch of her own label in 1993. She is credited as a pioneer of salvage fashion, with strong respect for craft.

She uses layering, handpainting and stitching techniques to create modern forms and is regarded by I-D magazine as one of the 150 most influential designers in the world.

Jessica's designs have been included in exhibitions in London, Prague, Antwerp and Tokyo. She was awarded the Vidal Sassoon Award for cutting Edge Talent in August 2002 and is considered Jamaica's most successful fashion designer.

# IVY RALPH – FASHION DESIGNER

Ivy Ralph, had the idea from childhood of a more comfortable dress style for black men. She desperately wanted men to move from European jacket-and-tie outfit, to something far more in tune with local climatic conditions.

In the 1970s, London was undoubtedly the fashion capital of the world. Women were against the status quo by wearing the shortest minis and hot pants. Jamaica could not be left out. In the spring of 1972, 10 years after the nation gained independence, Ivy Ralph, manager of the House of Ivy's and a graduate of the New York's Fashion Institute, staged a fashion show at her atelier then located at Central Avenue opposite The Queens High School. It was there that the 'Kareeba' was born.

The name was created to break all European connections. Government members, including then Prime Minister Michael Manley loved it and bought it. It became the rage. It was embraced by other ladies in the Caribbean and Africa. Errol Barrow, Prime Minister of Barbados, Forbes Burnham of Guyana, Julius Nyrere of Tanzania all got into the fashion. To this day, the Kareeba or Bush Jac still influences the way males in the Caribbean dress.

# Jaunel McKenzie - Model

Jaunel McKenzie, created history in New York in 2003 when she became the first Jamaican model to shoot American *Vogue*. Then, as a teenager, she had shot three *Vogues* in the space of two weeks. Jaunel and superstar Nadine Willis combined in 2003, had shot for all the major editions of *Vogue* for that year. These two ladies have certainly heralded the arrival of the Jamaicans on the international modelling scene.

By 2006, Jaunel was well within the top 30 models in the world and commanded a daily rate that is oftentimes more than what most models earn in a year. Certainly, from a financial and prestige point of view, Jaunel McKenzie is now the most successful model that the Caribbean region has produced.

The CEO of Pulse, Kingsley Cooper, who discovered Jaunel, had this to say: 'We are very proud of Jaunel. She is the perfect example of what a great work ethic, quiet confidence, intelligence and a winning personality can accomplish'.

# Carla Campbell – Model

Carla Campbell who was discovered by the Pulse model search became in 2006 the first model from the Caribbean to appear in the coveted annual swimsuit edition of *Sports Illustrated* magazine.

Carla has now joined the ranks of the select women of any colour who have graced the pages of the coveted publication, considered by many to be the most sought after job in fashion.

She started the climb to superstardom in 2005 when she copped a number of super editorials for *Cosmopolitan*, shot *Victoria Secret* and an *Esquire* cover. These prepared her for the break with *Sports Illustrated.*

Other Black models who have graced the pages of *Sports Illustrated* have been Noemie Lenoir, Loraine Pascale, Georgianna Robertson, Roshumba Williams, Jessica White and Tyra Banks.

# NADINE WILLIS – MODEL

Rephrasing the biblical dictum, 'can anything good come out of Ephesus?' to 'can anything good come out of Waterhouse?' the answer is yes, Nadine Willis the young lady who made the meteoric rise from 'Ghetto to Gucci'. Nadine has appeared in almost every important fashion magazine and six different Vogue publications – British, French, Italian, Japanese, German and Spanish. Her client list reads like a who's who of the market and continues to grow.

It is said that if you always do the things you always did you will get the same results. Nadine decided to break out of the box. She just strolled into Kingsley Cooper's office at Pulse Model Agency and told him she wanted to become the top model in the world. Kingsley Cooper was very impressed and took her to London and she was signed up by SELECT, one of the top agencies. Within four days she was doing the London fashion week, then French Vogue with Mario Testino who selected her two weeks later for the Gucci campaign.

Nadine, unlike several rags to riches persons, has a social conscience and has not forgotten her roots. Her determination to make a difference in the community in which she was raised has lead her to write a soon to be published book, *Stolen Childhood* which records her experiences growing up in Waterhouse.

Nadine has a history of making things happen rather than waiting for them to happen. She would from time to time go to the Balcombe Drive and Drews Avenue primary schools to give talks to the girls about teenage pregnancy. She said: 'I want to help a lot of other young girls to see the difference in themselves, to see that they can do more than what they require of themselves, because a lot of girls just think, ok yes, I'm gonna have a baby and that's it; that is not it – that is not what it is all about. You can do other stuff with your life.'

'Look at my life. It's like I was a girl living in Waterhouse, didn't even know I would get the chance to do all these things. Modeling has been the vehicle. It is nice because I have been to some fabulous places. I have traveled to many countries and I have enjoyed it. I have seen many nice people, like Iman. I wouldn't even dream of meeting Iman. I have actually worked with her. She is nice. I have even met Alek Wek and Naomi Campbell.'

Nadine admits that a lot has changed about her in the short while she has been in the spotlight. Going back to school and getting a proper education, one of the things a lack of proper family guidance prevented, is now one of her priorities.

# EDUCATION

# LEN GARRISON – EDUCATOR/COMMUNITY ACTIVIST

Len was born in Jamaica then migrated to England to further his education and pursue an academic career, graduating from Sussex University in African and Caribbean History. He later went to Rushkin College, Oxford, where he gained a diploma in Development Studies and Leicester University where he attained an MA in Local History. His achievements included, being founder member in the mid-60s of the International Social Group whose work led to the establishment of the Wandsworth Council for Community Relations. In 1977 he founded the Afro-Caribbean Resource Project (ACRP) to publish and produce learning materials drawn from the Black British experience for use in the school curriculum.

Len represented Britain at the 1977 Festival of Arts and Culture in Nigeria. He also lectured extensively on his work, in the UK and abroad. He also co-founded the Black Cultural Archives (BCA) in 1981. It houses documentary evidence of the Black presence and struggle, paying homage to the thousands who fought or those who lost their lives in the First and Second World Wars. BCA also works in partnership with Middlesex University and created the charitable organisation the Archives and Museum of Black Heritage (AMBH).

# Dr Marcia Keizs

Dr Marcia Keizs worked her way up administrative posts to become President of York College of City University New York (CUNY) January 24, 2005. She took up her new position at the Jamaica Queen's Campus, moving from Bronx Community College, another (CUNY) facility, where she was Vice-President of Academic Affairs since 1997.

York is a degree granting university with an approximate enrolment of 6,000 students. This appointment was the second stint at York College for Dr Keizs, who served the institution as acting president in 1996.

At the commission service held at the St Andrew Anglican Church in Hartsdale on Sunday February 13, 2006, Consul General to New York Dr Basil Bryan, described the appointment as a symbol of Jamaican spirit of excellence.

He said that Dr Keizs' achievement, 'was characteristic of the Jamaican spirit, one that is able to rise to the challenge thereby taking advantage of various opportunities, no matter where our people find themselves.'

Born in Kingston, Dr Keizs attended Ardenne and St Andrew High schools before migrating to Canada with her family. She moved to New York in 1968 and has held senior administrative posts at five CUNY colleges during a career spanning over three decades.

She is also the founding editor of the *New York Carib News* and has published articles on her area of specialty, Afro-American Literature.

# Dr Sylvia Whitlock

Sylvia Whitlock was on her way to her school principal job in the US when she heard the news on the radio that Supreme Court had just issued a ruling that a woman could become a member of a US Rotary club. Her club, Duarte, had previously tried to admit women and lost its charter as a result.

Two months later, when this Jamaican lady was sworn in as the installed club's president, she made history in Rotary by becoming the first woman president of a Rotary club.

Whitlock was born in New York of Jamaican parents then sent to Jamaica for early schooling. After High School, she returned to New York where she earned a bachelor's degree in psychology from Hunter Collage. After the birth of her son, she and her husband, a production manager for NBC television, moved to Pomona, California, where the mild climate reminded her of Jamaica.

Later on, Whitlock gave birth to another son and a daughter, earned a graduate and doctoral degrees in education, and became a school administrator in Duarte, an ethnically diverse town of 20,000 resting at the foot of the San Gabriel mountains, 20 miles north east of Los Angeles.

The Rotary club of Duarte was undergoing changes and growth of its own. In 1976, the club invited three women to join, a violation of Rotary International's policy at the time. The club's charter was revoked in 1978 and a lawsuit was filed. The case made its way through the legal system until the Supreme Court decided the matter. In 1989, the Rotary International council on legislation voted to open club membership to women worldwide.

Dr Whitlock says she did not aspire to be club president, but she noted that in a small club almost everyone got a chance at the office sooner or later. Her turn just happened to have come during that landmark year.

# LORD WILLIAM MORRIS OF HANDSWORTH

Lord Morris, although retired, continues to contribute to both the governance of Britain and tertiary education in Jamaica. He sits as a non-executive member on the Board of the Bank of England, he was recently appointed to head a special commission to evaluate the workings of the metropolitan police, and he is, at the same time, Chancellor of University of Technology, Jamaica.

Lord Morris is from the parish of Manchester and he left his homeland more than fifty years ago to seek an education and a new life in England. He got both and today is regarded in England as a leading standard bearer of the modern British trade union movement. As the general secretary of the Transport and General Workers Union, he ushered in a new era to the largest and most powerful labour union in England.

Lord Morris, has become only the second man of colour to rise to such eminence. He followed the legendary Sir Learie Constantine, iconic figure in West Indies cricket, the first of our Caribbean to be so honoured. William 'Bill' Morris broke down many barriers, especially prejudice in trade unionism and created a more equitable life at the workplace, not just for himself but for the British of all races.

# RONALD BLAKE

Ronald Blake, who was born in Jamaica, went to Canada in 1966. He is the founder and Director of Studies of the Higher Marks Educational Institute Inc, in Toronto. The Institute specializes in remedial and intervention education and addresses the needs of students who face academic, self-esteem and self-confidence problems in the regular school system.

Over its more than 23 years history, more than 6,000 students have been assisted. Higher Marks, whose impact on education has been the subject of TV documentaries on CBC, CTV, WTN, Sask. – TV and Rogers Cable, is also the creator of the Prophonics self–help reading system. Blake is also a leading lecturer on Black history.

He is credited with writing the following: *How to Motivate the Student*; (booklets); *Jamaica: Great Nation, Great Problems, Great Future* (1999); *Ruler in the Kingdom of Men* (1991).

He also received several honours, including: People of Excellence Award; Harry Jerome Award for Professional Excellence; Certificate for contribution in the field of Education; Award for service to the community.

# Claudette Bruccoleri

Claudette, Jamaican–born, migrated to Canada in 1980. She joined the Calgary Board of Education as a teacher. Claudette is the creator of and facilitator of a Social Justice Education course, which is being taught at Queen Elizabeth Junior Secondary School in Calgary, with the aim of increasing awareness and acceptance of people from diverse ethno–cultural and religious backgrounds.

The course is possibly the only one of its kind being taught within the Calgary school system. Previously, she worked in establishing a private school for disadvantaged students and worked with a team of educators in Montreal in establishing the Greaves Academy. She is a member of the committee on Equity with the Calgary Board of Education; she is also a member of the ARUSHA Board of Calgary; a regular presenter on Women's health issues, in Montreal and Calgary. She has recently completed a paper on African-Canadian female leaders in education.

# Professor Erma Collins

She left Jamaica for Canada in 1960 with a teaching diploma. There she did further studies and became known as an educator and community volunteer. Professor Collins, who started her teaching career at the elementary level in Jamaica, retired in 1998 from George Brown College as Professor of Business English. During her tenure at George Brown College she was Chairperson of English and Liberal Studies Department. As chairperson, she monitored the development and delivery of 60 post-secondary courses in English, French and Social Sciences.

Despite her busy academic schedule, she found time to be involved in the community – a community involvement which started in Jamaica where she ran a community library, tutored students and taught basic English to adults. In Canada her community involvement included: Black Educator's Group; Executive, National Council of Jamaicans and Supportive Organization in Canada; Active supporter of the Provincial Liberal Association; Community Advisory Committee, B'nai Brith Canada.

Professor Collins has received honours including: Harry Jerome Award; Award of Merit, John Brooks Community Foundation; Urban Alliance Race Relations Award; Volunteer Appreciation Award. She has published several articles and a book, *Brush Up Your English* (1979).

# ENTREPRENEURS

# GEORGE STIEBEL

George Stiebel came from humble beginnings. His mother was a housekeeper and his father a Jew from Hamburg in Germany. He had some schooners which were involved in gun-running in the Caribbean, especially in Cuba, which in the 1840s was still a slave colony. He was aboard one of the schooners which sank off the coast of Venezuela, but he was able to swim ashore.

Although distraught when he realized that he had lost everything, Stiebel did not give up. With the money he rescued, he bought goods and became a peddlar. He was immensely successful, especially in buying gold and transporting it to Caracas. Over the years, he gained an insight into the mining of gold, and when he heard that the Venezuelan government was interested in leasing an old mine, El Callo, George persuaded some friends to become partners. He put all his capital in this venture.

When some of his partners lost heart, he bought them out and persevered with determination. He later found gold. The mine was valued at US$16M, one fourth of which belonged to Stiebel. He came back to Jamaica a wealthy man.

In 1891 he was decorated with the order of St Michael at St George by Queen Victoria. He later bought Devon Pen and constructed Devon House. Devon House became the envy of the rich and famous in Jamaica. However, Lady Musgrave, wife of the Governor General was so incensed by it that she refused to pass by the house owned by a Black man, which was grander than Kings House. As a result, her husband built Lady Musgrave Road in order to bypass Devon House.

# Anita Witter

Entrepreneur Anita Witter received the silver award at the British Female Inventor and Innovative Network (BFIIN) awards in the 'exceptionally creative' category, for her development of Jewel Isle Rum Punch. Although she was told about the BFIIN programme, she was reluctant to enter because she did not think the competition was for her.

The organizers contacted her again and expressed their disappointment that she had not sent in her application. With that sort of encouragement, she had no choice but to send it in. The awards which took place at the Guildhall in London, gave women across the United Kingdom an opportunity to exhibit their inventions and innovative ideas and products.

Witter said of her award: 'For me, it is a great achievement because the competition was very stiff. I did not expect that my innovation in creating the flavours of the Jewel Isle Rum Punch would have won, but the judges were impressed with the product.'

Jewel Isle Rum Punch was officially launched in 2005 at the Jamaican High Commission in London. It featured three flavours – tropical pineapple, ginger and lemon-lime. It is made with fruit juice and authentic white over-proof Jamaican rum.

# Kingsley Cooper

Kingsley Cooper the Jamaican Attorney-at-law, with an eye for beauty was honoured for consistently discovering and grooming models to dominate the international catwalks. In August 2005 he was honoured in New York for his pioneering role in the development of Caribbean's modeling, fashion and entertainment industries. He was awarded a star at the inaugural Reggae Red Carpet awards in Manhattan at the Ritzy Spirit nightclub.

Cooper conceived and developed the Caribbean Fashion centre PULSE in New Kingston as well as the nine-acre Eco-friendly Villa Ronai Project in Stony Hill, Jamaica. On hand to share the occasion in New York were Vogue and Gucci models Nadine Willis and Jaunel McKenzie, Pulse's then, latest international modeling stars, amongst a host of celebrities.

Mr. Cooper said:

> 'After 25 years of hard work, in the process succeeding repeatedly at what so many thought could not be done, it is good to have my work finally recognized and my vision appreciated.'

The citation honouring Cooper said in part, 'Mr. Kingsley Cooper, an attorney, gave up his law practice to found Pulse 25 years ago. He has been chairman and CEO ever since and has pioneered the development of the modeling and fashion business in the Caribbean. Under his guidance Pulse has produced several world class models and beauty queens through its modeling agency and the Caribbean Model Search. He has also developed Caribbean Fashion Week, regarded by Vogue as a hot new trend in world fashion.

# Michael Lee Chin

Michael Lee Chin migrated to Canada in the 1960s and became one of that country's most successful entrepreneurs. He was presented with an outstanding Philanthropist award by the Association of Fundraising Professionals, Greater Toronto Chapter in November 2005.

As a Jamaican who was never afraid to think out of the box, he demonstrated that quality when he was studying – he did not have the funds to pay his school fees so he wrote to the then Prime Minister of Jamaica, Hugh Lawson Shearer, made a very convincing case for funding, with a caveat that he would 'give' back to Jamaica. He was successful. He went on to complete his degree in Civil Engineering, worked at a number of jobs before joining the financial industry in 1977.

In 1983, Lee Chin invested $500,000 in the McKenzie Financial Corporation; by 1987, the investment was worth $3.5million. Two years later, with the gains from his investment, he founded his own financial services company, the Berkshire Group. Then, in 1986, he purchased a small Hamilton-based investment firm, Advantage Investment Council (AIC), which offered at the time, only one fund, AIC Advantage Fund, and held assets of about $800,000. Today AIC has over $14 billion under management by using the investment principle 'Buy, Hold, and Prosper' and from investing in the wealth management industry, he has added more than 40 funds to the company's portfolio.

In 2002 Lee Chin purchased 75 percent ownership in one of Jamaica's leading banks, the National Commercial Bank (NCB). He has also purchased businesses in Barbados and Trinidad and Tobago.

# LOWELL HAWTHORNE

Lowell Hawthorne, a highly successful Jamaican – born entrepreneur, has piloted Golden Krust Caribbean Bakery and grill from a small New York bakery to become one of the leading ready-to-eat Caribbean food franchises in the US, with more than 100 stores nationwide. Golden Krust made its name selling traditional Jamaican specialties such as patties, buns and turnovers, and now offers Reggaefest meals such as jerk chicken and fish.

In 1995, *Forbes* Magazine featured Golden Krust as one of the fastest growing minority-owned business in the US and in 2002, Hawthorne was named 'Entrepreneur of the Year' for the tri-state area by the accounting firm Ernst & Young.

Hawthorne made his first patty at age 11 at Hawthorne and Sons bakery, the family's business in Lawrence Tavern St Andrew. He developed his entrepreneurial spirit as a child, rearing and selling pigs and chicken. Later he did a stint driving a minibus between Lawrence Tavern and Half-Way-Tree.

In the early 1980s, he left the bus job to move with his parents and, eventually, his 11 siblings to the US. Their father, Ephraim, opened the first Golden Krust in 1989 on Gun Hill Road in the Bronx, with the hope of bringing the traditional Jamaican food to their fellow migrants.

At first Hawthorne and his siblings busied themselves with school and sought traditional jobs. He chose accounting since he was always good with figures. However, a few years later, he gave way to his entrepreneurial urges and left his job as an accountant with the police force to enter the family business full time. Under his leadership, Gun Hill Road has become the flagship store of a network of more than 100 franchises across the United States.

In 2004, the company struck its first major endorsement contract, signing New York Jets Star Tiki Barber. Hawthorne is the first to admit that the key to success is keeping the company's roots firmly planted in the Caribbean community. Linkages have been established with the Jamaica Agricultural Society, the Ministry of Agriculture and the Jamaica Exporters' Association (JEA) in a collaborative venture for the purpose of producing particular crops to supply the chain.

# Denham Jolly

Denham Jolly had an early prosperity lesson from his father: 'It is always better to work for yourself than for others'. Notwithstanding, Denham found he had to work for someone else at first to save up some capital before starting on his own journey to prosperity and history. As such he worked in Jamaica in nutrition for a while before migrating to Canada. In Canada he became a successful real estate magnate then the owner of Canada's only black-owned commercial radio station.

After studying at McGill University, Jolly was teaching physics and chemistry at a private Toronto High School when he realized that racism would impede his progress there. Because of that strong sense of self with which he left Jamaica, he was a no–nonsense person. He moved on using a CDN $5,000 loan to purchase an accommodation for student rental near the University of Toronto. When that did well, he acquired other properties, started a nursing home at which point he gave up teaching. At one time, his holdings included apartment buildings, medical labs, a hotel and a 20–metre yacht running day trips out of Montego Bay.

However, it was his participation in the city's prominent black organizations that led to his current role as president and CEO of FLOW 93:5 FM. He fought housing discrimination, advocated police accountability and was instrumental in the community's 12-year battle to win a FM license. In 2001, the Jolly-led Milestone Radio Inc. became Canada's first urban format radio station. Jolly's advice to budding entrepreneurs: 'Dream in colour and stick to it'.

# Ainsley Harriott – Chef/TV Personality

Ainsley Harriott, with his trademark ear-to-ear smile, is a celebrity chef in the United Kindgom, with several popular television shows – Good Morning with Ann and Nick, Can't Cook, Won't Cook and later Ready, Steady, Cook – that have endeared him to fans outside of the UK. He is also an author with bestselling cookbooks and has his own line of food including couscous, soups and cereal bars. The exuberant chef's passionate journey to fame and success can be credited in part to his solid West Indian upbringing, which included accessing the recipes and acquiring the tastes of several 'aunts' and 'uncles' from a very diverse immigrant community, and the atmosphere of singing, dancing and laughter that possessed the Harriott's home.

In 1952, Ainsley's father, Chester Harriott, left the shores of Jamaica to take up a scholarship to the Royal School of Music – unheard of for a Black man in those days – and became a famous pianist in his own right making appearances on the very popular [at the time] Bob Monkhouse Show and also as a guest on the Ed Sullivan Show in the United States. Chester later met Peppy, Ainsley's mother who was also Jamaican, in London where she was working as a nurse. According to Vicky Allan in a 2002 feature on the top chef, 'The immigrant identity has always been a part of what [Ainsley] Harriott is about, right back to when he used to be part of a singing duo called the Calypso Twins'…with Paul Boross and released a record in the early 1990s, 'World Party', which was a major hit.

Trained at Westminster College of Catering, Ainsley obtained an apprenticeship at Verrey's restaurant in the West End and later worked as a commis (trainee) chef. He became head chef at Lord's Cricket's Ground Long Room and was asked to present More Nosh, Less Dosh on BBC Radio 5. Harriott has worked as a chef in London hotels and restaurants including the Dorchester, Brown's, The Hilton, The Westbury, Café Pelican and Quaglino's.

In September 2008, Harriott took part in the genealogy documentary series *Who Do You Think You Are*, in the quest to find out more about his family history. He was able to trace his family connection to the island of Jamaica back by five generations – to Hamilton Forbes and Catherine Smith, who married there in 1846.

# MARCIA BROWN

Before leaving Jamaica, Marcia Brown helped in a significant way to build the brands of companies like Johnson and Johnson, Colgate–Palmolive, Nabisco and Coca-Cola for 16 years. Today, the Jamaican-born marketing executive is the CEO of her own Atlanta-based marketing firm, The Monarch Group.

In 2000, the company where she worked restructured and her career took a backward step. She was uncomfortable so she settled her nerves and rang the company's senior vice president and told him how she could better serve the company. Impressed with her winning attitude, the VP put her in charge of an important in-house project: one that put the very self–confident manager in the direct eye–line of the company president. She did extremely well with the project and the president was impressed with her work.

That was the kind of bravado that led Marcia Brown to take the plunge and launch The Monarch Group in 2003, a consumer marketing company specializing in personal branding for high potential executives. When a company president with a struggling product and no branding strategy calls, Brown deploys members of her virtual team of experts based on that executive's specific needs. It is not only an efficient way to work, Brown maintained, but by substituting office–bound employees for off -site workers, Monarch also saves the clients a lot of fixed expenses since she does the work on a one-off basis.

When she is not attending speaking engagements or brokering deals for Monarch, Marcia is writing. She has co–authored two personal branding books, *Brand Me Inc* and *Brand Me at Work*, both of which she sells on her website Monarchbiz.net. It is part of the strategy to grow her business on a number of fronts.

# CHRISTOPHER HOHN – PHILANTHROPIST

The Jamaican parents of Chris Hohn immigrated to England in 1960. His father Paul, is a retired motor mechanic. Chris showed brilliance at a young age; he was successful in 13 'O' levels and was a top footballer at the same time. Chris Hohn later graduated from Southampton University. This brilliant student went on to study at Harvard University where he was in the top 5 per cent of his MBA class.

On graduation from Harvard Business School, he began his career in finance on Wall Street. Then, in 2003, he went out on his own and set up the Children's Investment Fund Foundation. Today, his hedge fund is one of the most successful in Europe.

The Children's Investment was set up to donate a fixed proportion (1%) of its profits to its charitable arm – the Children's Investment Fund Foundation. Hohn was influenced to structure his business that way when he saw children scavenging for food in the Philippines. The foundation is run by his wife, Jamie and has given money to the Clinton Foundation for the treatment of HIV/AIDS; and to emergency aid projects in places such as Darfur.

In four years, up to 2008, his fund has given away almost £800 million, making Chris Hohn Britain's largest giver. In fact, in 2008, he gave away over £500 million in donation which makes it the largest single donation ever made in the UK. Today, Christopher Hohn is in the top three of the high earners in the top ten city earners in London.

# Jennifer and Lloyd Samuda

Jencare started in a 12x12 room then as it expanded it opened in the Red Hills Mall then expanded again until it has its own spa in spacious surroundings in Hope Road in Kingston, Trinidad, Miami and New York.

Jencare is, most of all, famous for a line of skin care products for black skin developed by Jennifer Samuda, which are now marketed worldwide. Lloyd Samuda, her husband, is the not–so–visible half of the Jencare partnership which has given Jamaica an international name in beauty care.

Sixteen years ago, Lloyd Samuda left a very promising career in agriculture and project management to dedicate himself full time to the family business. His wife left her job in banking to do the same. Family members could not believe they were serious: 'they asked how could we leave our good jobs for something which was so uncertain.'

The couple started manufacturing at home as Jennifer's co-workers began asking her for what she used on her skin that was obviously so effective. Of course, Mrs. Samuda went back to school and took courses in cosmetology, too, and soon her services as a skin care consultant were in high demand.

Among Jencare Skin Farm's many achievements are the European award for quality (1999), the environmental management award in gold category in 2000 and the same award presented a year later in the platinum category.

# Captain Horace Burrell

The final of the world cup of football is reserved for giants, not dwarfs. Yet Captain Horace Burrell dreamt that he could take this little country of Jamaica to engage the Goliaths of world football! The Captain's big dreams were not limited to the army and football but extended to his business ventures.

By 1985, Cake World, the family business was doing extremely well and had expanded beyond its cottage industry status. He had to make a life changing decision to leave the army and invest more time in the business in order for it to grow even more. They now had stores in Kingston, Spanish Town and May Pen. However, when he and his wife separated, she kept the business name and he took his assets and formed the Captain's Bakery. The first one was located in downtown Kingston where Burrell fostered a wonderful relationship with the staff and the community. The business soon expanded to Crossroads, New Kingston, May Pen, Montego Bay and Grand Cayman.

In 1994, Burrell was elected President of the Jamaica Football Federation (JFF) and set about immediately to revamp Jamaican football. His plan was to take Jamaica to the World Cup in France in 1998. He had a PowerPoint presentation of his plans and a budget of $104 million which included hiring a Brazilian coach. He went for a meeting with then Prime Minister P.J. Patterson and won him over.

Once the world cup qualification matches began, Burrell became aware that the locally based players had gone as far as they could and were facing elimination. Burrell then turned to England and recruited Jamaican born English football club players.

On November 17, 1997, Jamaica and Mexico met at 'the office' – Jamaica National Stadium. All Jamaica needed was a draw for the unthinkable to happen. The game ended 0-0 and Jamaica was in the finals of France 1998. Burrell's dream had become a reality! Sensing that this was a moment like no other, and remembering how he had kept faith with one determined Jamaican who had a vision, The government declared the following day, Monday, a national holiday to mark this achievement.

# Neil Seaton

Seaton, principal and chairman of Diamond Paints, helped his company to develop a wall treatment product for which it entered into distribution negotiations with a large US hardware chain that would immediately make the local product available throughout that country.

The product, a calcium-based veneer plaster that is used in the construction industry to prepare surfaces before painting, will be manufactured in Jamaica under the diamond brand and retailed in the hardware chain throughout the USA. The product is made from 95 percent indigenous material.

Diamond Paints market outside of Jamaica has so far been confined to the Caribbean, where the brand is slowly beginning to gain a foothold. The company has exported to Antigua, Trinidad and Barbados.

Seaton noted that the product was very versatile with application in both cold and warm weather, and was ideally suited for the North American market.

At least one other Diamond Paint product has already received world acceptance. The company's plaster filler is packaged and branded for a world-renowned, German-based chemical company and sold internationally. As such, the company is more of a designer of specialized products for the construction industry rather than simply a paint manufacturer.

# RODNEY DAVIS

Rodney Davis was born off Hagley Park Road in Kingston but spent most of his life in Canada before destiny brought him back home in July 2005 to head Cable and Wireless Jamaica. He enjoyed one of the most successful phases of his life at the helm of a multinational company in his homeland. He left that company in 2007 and purchased a men's haircare business.

When he left Jamaica in 1968 with his mother to live in Canada he never lost his roots. Jamaican culture remained an integral part of his life. He still had his Saturday soup, fish on Sundays and the sounds of reggae music in the community.

Later on, in Canada, Jamaican–born Davis became President and one of the founders of Nappy's Inc., a chain of hair salons. Nappy's was founded in 1999 with a mission to improve the service and quality of men's and women's haircare services in Toronto; the company now has five locations throughout south western Ontario.

Davis began his career at KPMG Peat Marwick Throne, 1989-1995, as senior audit consultant and manager in corporate finance, mergers and acquisitions. In 1995, he left KPMG and joined Southam Inc., Canada's largest newspaper publishers. Soon he was appointed vice-president finance and corporate controller responsible for all aspects of the company's accounting, financing and treasury, including public financial reporting, business plan approval, capital budgets and newspaper acquisitions. While at Southam, he was instrumental in the negotiation and purchase of the *Financial Post* and the *National Post* newspapers.

He later joined Maxxcom Inc., where he served as vice-president, corporate development, planning and executing the company's corporate development programme and leading the acquisition for Cybersight, while taking the company public on the Toronto Stock Exchange. In 2000, he joined MGI, a provider of visual media software products and infrastructure as their Chief Financial Officer (CFO).

# Patrick Sibbles

Patrick Sibbles, with an investment of US$250,000, established another of his trademark coffee shops, The Coffee Mill of Jamaica in China on March 31, 2006. This venture is Jamaica's first totally foreign–owned investment in China. The opening of the café, which sells authentic Blue Mountain Coffee, was described by Jamaica's ambassador to China as 'the first shot across the bow at those who attempt to undermine Blue Mountain Coffee.'

Coffee can only accurately be labelled 'Blue Mountain' if it is grown in the 28-mile eastern mountain range, and in specific areas of St Thomas and Portland. The beans must be grown above 2,000 feet.

Cups of the brew, marketed as authentic Blue Mountain coffee, are available in some of China's major cities. The Coffee Mill's Pudong location, however, has gone one step further, changing a corner of a hotel lobby into a little piece of Jamaica. They set the scene with Africa inspired art, reggae music playing softly in the background, shelves lined with Walkers Wood spices and seasoning and, of course, the familiar brown bags of Blue Mountain Coffee. Located on the first floor of the upscale Tong Mao Hotel, the Coffee Mill café opened its doors a little over a year after initial links were made during the China Caribbean economic and trade fair in 2005.

Sibbles said: 'We are not really new kids on the block. We have had this vision from the beginning, and after 30 years it has culminated into today.'

# Kemeel Azan

Kemeel Azan was born in Jamaica but migrated to Canada in 1958. Kemeel has been living his dreams – the hair business – over 40 years now. He lived it as an educator, business owner, and stylist He opened his first salon in 1962 and by 1972 he owned and operated salons in four locations across Toronto, including Yorkville, and had a staff of 42 employees.

He is known for his high standards, skill in service delivery and business development practices. A number of leading hair stylists currently operating their own establishments in Toronto had trained or worked with him earlier in their careers. His salon is the one of choice by Blacks in and around Toronto. Always interested in training and development, he used his business experience to benefit others: he wrote a manual on 'How to Run a Small Business', which was accepted into the school system, provides mentoring opportunities to secondary school students in his salons, speaks to and encourages youths on the importance of education and career choices. Indeed he has helped shape the careers of a number of young, aspiring individuals.

He has been involved in the community in a number of other ways including: promoter of the annual Cotillion Ball; spearheaded the purchase and restoration of two Toronto Churches on behalf of the Church of God of Prophecy; was a member of the Milestone Radio's lobbying team, which submitted briefs to the CRTC for the granting of a license to what is now FLOW 93.5 FM – first Black-owned radio station in Canada.

Azan has received a number of awards, including: Awards from Hair News magazine, New York, Philadelphia, Detroit and Washington. He also received the Beauty Industry Pioneer Award.

# Dr Carlton Braithwaite

Carlton was born in Jamaica then migrated to Canada in 1962. This former athlete and mathematics teacher has extensive experience in the Canadian public and private sectors. From 1966 he worked for the federal government, serving as Chief, Econometric Research Division, Statistics Canada, then as Senior Economist, Economic Council of Canada. During this time he authored over 30 papers and several studies and books, a number of which led to changes in methodologies at Statistics Canada, the Economic Council and elsewhere as well as influenced government practices and policies.

He also established himself as one of the leading economists on investment in Canada. In 1983, he moved to the private sector where he formed and presided over the Uniprop Group of Companies, which invested mainly in real estate and high tech industries. In a very short time the group amassed holdings in excess of $100 million.

In 1987, he co–founded the Commonwealth Club of Ottawa, later renamed Commonwealth Club International, an international business and social club. During 1995-97, he also served as a member of the Board of Directors of Ontario Reality Corp. and as an Associate of the Glen Ardith–Frazer Corp., an independent investment management company.

He is affiliated with a number of community organizations which include: City of Ottawa Advisory Group on Visible Minorities; Consultative Group for Black Canadian Studies Chair at Dalhousie University; Alumni President, Ottawa Coronary Health Improvement Program; Director, Executive Board, Queen's University Alumni Association.

Among his publications are several papers, studies and books; 'The Impact of Investment Incentives on Canada's Economic Growth', (1983); 'An Econometric Analysis of the Determinants of Investment in Canadian Manufacturing,' (1971).

Among the honours he has received are several athletic and academic awards, including Skelton Clarke Fellowship and Queen's University Inaugural Harry Jerome Business Award, 1990.

# WELLS DAVIS

Davis has been in Canada since 1967 and before establishing his own company – Clarity and Urban Engines, he was head of the Strategy Department of Canada's largest advertising and communications agency, McLaren McCann. He and his team were responsible for developing communications strategy for some of Canada's largest companies, including General Motors (GM), Royal Bank, Microsoft, Rogers Cable, Nissan, Apple, Ford, Xerox, and The Toronto Zoo.

The strategies developed were then used in the development of television, print, magazine, internet, promotions, and direct mail communications. In addition to his expertise in advertising, he is also a professional researcher; prior to joining McLaren McCann, he spent three years with DesRosiers Automotive Research as a Senior Consultant and Managing Editor. There, he conducted industry forecasts and wrote a newsletter on the automotive industry. He regularly conducts primary research for his advertising clients. Davis has appeared on CBC News World and CBC Radio as an expert on advertising.

He has received several honours including: Contribution to Award-winning campaigns for clients such as Toronto Zoo, Rogers Cable, GM, Ford, Nissan and Shoppers Drug Mart.

# DENZIL FERGUSON

Denzil Ferguson has been credited with inventing the Fercon building system, a system that quickly, efficiently and easily lays blocks compared to the time consuming line cord method commonly used. Ferguson was practically born into construction, growing up in the business beside his father, also a block manufacturer. He later added to his hands-on experience gained at his father's workplace, by enrolling in a block-making technology class at Clarke College in Vancouver, Washington. Mr. Ferguson worked for six years with Columbia Block Machines, one of the largest manufactures of block-making equipment.

His interest in construction mellowed when he pursued an Associates Degree in Agricultural Sciences at the College of Agricultural Sciences (CASE). He did a course in engineering which triggered the interest

Mr. Ferguson, a former president of the Block Manufacturers' Association for 13 years, invented the polished block when he was in his twenties but never patented it because he was unaware of the importance of intellectual property rights. He took the idea to an international company and 10 years later the company built a machine to mass-produce these blocks. He learnt from his mistake and got a patent on the new invention.

The Fercon method is a conveyer type block-laying system. It saves as much as twenty percent on time, efficiency and building costs.

# Andrew Lewis

Andrew Lewis was made redundant by the University of Technology and that cranked up his inventive juices in 2003. He invented a doll called Rasbot. It is a miniature-sized doll that can dance to any Bob Marley tune and kick a football with similar agility as the late King of Reggae. In his back pocket, there is a red handkerchief and he wears on his feet a pair of brown sandals. The doll has locks and wore a colourful attire consisting of red, green and gold.

The inventor is a member of the Innovators' Association which falls under the Scientific Research Council (SRC). He said he got the inspiration for the invention one day as he walked through the Craft Market in Ocho Rios, St Ann where he saw several attractive dolls which he thought would have more impact on the tourism market with just a bit of added technology. Lewis came up with his first invention in 1985 when he invented a coin-operated train which went around the track, through a tunnel once with a 10 cent coin deposited in a reception box.

In December 2002, he also invented another toy, Grandfather, using infrared technology. Like Rasbot, Grandfather is a male doll armed with a flag in his left hand and will recite the national pledge and sing the national anthem at the touch of a button.

Mr. Lewis has since contacted a game development company in order to further develop the dancing doll.

# DR HALDEN MORRIS

Dr Halden Morris, in charge of Technical and Vocational Education at the Institute of Education, The University of the West Indies, Mona Campus, invented a portable clothes dryer in 2005 for which he secured a US patent that same year. The device works from electricity mains and features a telescopic rectangular outer drum and cylindrical inner drum. It measures 18 inches by 18 inches and weighs 20 pounds and designed to fit in a suitcase. The device operates like a fan heater and can dry two daysworth of clothes in 30 minutes.

Dr Morris said the idea originated with a suggestion by a friend, Rhona Miller, with whom he shares the patent. She asked him to find a solution for her wet clothes and hair during her travels when she is without a dryer. This invention was not his first, but it was the first to receive a US patent, having learnt the hard way. In 1984 he had come up with a technique to strengthen the front ball on an IBM typewriter but it was not patented.

He traveled and saw his idea being used but could not claim royalties because he had not protected his intellectual property rights. At the time of writing, he was finalizing negotiations with a Miami-based company for the manufacture and marketing of the product.

# IAN RANDLE - PUBLISHER

Ian Randle Publishers (IRP) was founded by Ian Randle who went into the field of publishing at age 21 when he left university. Prior to that he had spent over 15 years establishing Heinemann Caribbean as the leading educational publisher in the English-speaking Caribbean. Today, IRP is a medium sized publishing house producing some 50 titles a year and ranked as the leading publishers of Caribbean books anywhere in the world.

By 2005 the company had over 300 books in print at which time Randle transferred the active running of the business to his daughter Christine who had joined the company some years earlier from the legal profession. Since then he has remained behind the scenes developing special book projects, assisting in strategic planning as well as passing on the wisdom of 35years in the industry.

Mr. Randle told his story himself;

> 'In 1990 I never had any vision or ambition about starting my own business but I constantly needed to reinvent myself, and after 15 years with Heinemann I was getting restless. On the spur of the moment I decided to take the bold move to leave and set up my own business. Publishing was not well established; I had no backing and I chose the area of scholarly and academic publishing that no one had gone into before.
>
> People said there was no market for those kinds of books in Jamaica and the Caribbean. We created the marketing for writers and buyers. We help create opportunities for academics to express themselves and be able to gain international recognition. Publishing is highly capital-intensive and long–term, but two of the greatest assets when starting a business are contacts and a good reputation. I had developed a range of contacts regionally and internationally and was able to call on them.'

# WILFRED EMANUEL-JONES

Wilfred Emanuel-Jones was born in 1957 in the rural community of Frankfield, high up in the hills of Clarendon, Jamaica. He left the hills of rural Clarendon with his parents in search of a better life in Birmingham, England. That better life did not come easily. He, his parents and eight younger siblings had to live in a small house without the basic comforts which they were promised.

Emanuel-Jones has proven what a focused, determined and ambitious son of the soil can achieve anywhere in the world. He has braved the bad weather, the obvious prejudices and achieved beyond expectations to establish one of the United Kingdom's most successful farms, making millions of pounds yearly.

The frustrations he experienced at school and in the community, in general, resulted in very poor results at school. He graduated without any qualifications. However, he decided to make up for it when he joined the British Army. That stint did not last long because of his indiscipline. He was dismissed from the army. That was the best thing that ever happened to him. He realized then that success would come only with being focused, hard work and discipline.

He enrolled in a catering school and became a certified Chef. Fired with a passion to succeed he launched out on his first entrepreneurial venture - a restaurant. After a while, he decided that this was not illuminating enough for him so he went into television through the British Broadcasting Corporation (BBC) as a producer/ director of documentaries to do with food and beverages from all over the world for 15 years.

He later established a food and drink marketing company which earned him the capital to pay for his 40-acre farm in the hills of Devon, near Cornwall. Most people in the neighbourhood had never seen a black person before. They just could not understand why a black man wanted to purchase a farm. Little did they know that it was part of the DNA of the inhabitants in Frankfield in the hills of Clarendon. Noticing his driving ambition, they nicknamed him the 'Black Farmer'.

Emanuel-Jones rears sheep, cattle, pigs and has a food processing business where he produces a range of sausages, roasted chicken and a variety of food sauces under the 'Black Farmer' brand. He currently turns over more than £2 million in sales, yearly.

# Barrington Irving

Barrington Irving's story is steeped in destiny. His family relocated to Miami, USA from Jamaica when he was six, and it was there years later that he met a black airline pilot from Jamaica, Captain Gary Robinson. Irving who had never seen a Black pilot before was prompted to ask Robinson if he was a rocket scientist. Robinson responded: 'I am not a rocket scientist, and if I can do it, you can too'. Gary Robinson unwittingly ignited the fuel that would lead to a history-making aerial adventure. They developed a strong bond, driven by shared love of flying and strong Christian beliefs.

Gary Robinson took Irving to see a Boeing 777. The then 15 year-old was mesmerised. He turned down college football scholarships in order to pursue his dream to become a pilot. Barrington Irving has proven that it does not matter where you are from; it is where you plan to go which is of real importance. He started off in the innercity by washing aeroplanes. He tried to convince corporations that a young man could construct his own plane and fly around the world and he was the man to do it. He logged hundreds of miles attending air shows around the United States trying to enchant sponsors, but there were no takers. However, like any pioneer worth his salt, Irving never lost hope.

At age 21, Irving founded Experience Aviation Inc., a non-profit organization designed to motivate youth and address the significant shortage of younger, technically skilled professionals in aviation, aerospace, and other related career fields. Later on, the 23 year-old aerospace student built his own plane from more than US$300,000 in donated parts, took off from Miami on March 23, 2007 hoping to become the youngest person and the first black pilot to fly solo around the globe. He had planned to do so from 2006 but a lack of funding delayed his US$1million project.

His plane is dotted with small stickers with the flags of several of the countries he visited, including Spain, Italy, Greece and Japan. Irving's 26,000 mile trip included stops in Cleveland and New York before passing into Canada, then crossing the Atlantic, through Europe, the Middle East and Asia. Indeed, he traversed four continents, clocking more than 130 hours in flight time on a 97-day 'World Flight Adventure'.

On his return from his historic flight around the globe, Irving was labelled 'Superman' by Miami-Dade County Commissioner, Barbara Jordan. She presented him with the keys to the City and proclaimed June 27, 2007 'Barrington Irving Day'. At the ceremony, Jamaica's then Minister of Tourism, Entertainment and Culture, Aloun Assamba, read a poem 'Jamaica Wanderers'. 'When Barrington Irving decided to fly around the world, he was following in a deep Jamaican tradition'. She said Jamaicans have always soared to great heights and he has done so with distinction. All Jamaica is proud of this extraordinary son of the soil who has brought glory to his country and who has demonstrated what Jamaicans can achieve.

Irving is now studying at Florida Memorial University; he has private and commercial pilot licenses. He also founded Experience Aviation, a Miam-based organization that encourages minority youths to pursue aviation careers. Barrington Irving has proven that 'he who dares, wins'.

# Law and Medicine

# PATRICK CAMPBELL - LAW

Patrick was born and spent his most formative years in one of the worst areas in Kingston – close to Wareika Hill, Jarrett Lane, Jacques Road and other warring neighbourhoods. As such, his vivid recollection of childhood is not a pleasant one. As a young nine year-old during the 1980 election, he saw brutal violence and death unfold before his young eyes.

He attended Central Branch All-Age school, then Jamaica College where he made it to fourth form and was doing accelerated Mathematics and English when he left for the US in 1986 to join his mother.

Campbell then took a Street Law class which allowed him to participate in a mock trial competition in front of real judges in a real courtroom. His team won the competition, which was among all public high schools in Washington DC. It was then, at age 15, that he decided he would become a lawyer. He never let go of that dream.

Patrick is the third black man and the first Jamaican to partner in the US-based firm of Paul, Weiss, Rifkind, Wharton & Garrison LLP, a company of 500 lawyers with roots going back to 1875.

Once there, he made good use of the opportunities that presented themselves and he ended up at Georgetown University in Washington DC. After graduating from Georgetown he went to one of the top three law schools – Stanford – to read law. He was awarded the Carl Mason Franklin Prize for the most outstanding paper in the field of international law. A sage of old said the best way to motivate someone is to put him with a successful person. Campbell met a successful black corporate lawyer who had gone to his high school, and that planted the seed in his head that anything was possible.

# Pamela Appelt - Law

Pamela Appelt had a driving ambition to reach the top so when she reached England, she studied microbiology and biochemistry. She then migrated to Canada in 1966, and by 1987 she became the first Black woman to be appointed to the Court of Canadian Citizenship, a position she held until her retirement in 2000.

In Canada, she first worked as a biochemist at Queen Elizabeth Hospital in Montreal. She later worked as a researcher in medical biochemistry at McGill University for several years. The main themes in her life are to help children and families to have better lives; she speaks regularly to groups and organizations on issues of violence against women and children; she also speaks on issues concerning recent immigrants and visible minority women.

In 1999, she was appointed by the province of Ontario as a member of the Custody Review Board, which deals with young offenders. She is heavily involved in the community: the Clarke Institute of Psychiatry; York University; The Board of United Way, Advisor to the President of Northern Caribbean University; honoured by the Friends of Ron Hubbard Society for her outstanding community work and achievement.

# Dr Graham Sergeant - Medicine

In 1966, Dr Graham Sergeant, a new registrar in the Department of Medicine at UWI was invited to assist in the Sickle Cell Unit which was started in 1965 by Dr Paul Milner. A two-year grant was secured from the Wellcome Trust in London to study the natural history of the Sickle Cell disease in Jamaica.

A Volkswagen minibus was converted to a mobile clinical unit which was a vital part of the early research. It was used to help trace the many patients aged 30 years, who had not been seen at the University Hospital for periods up to 12 years. The assumption then was that these patients had died. However, over half were located in good health, reporting improvements with age. This study identified 60 patients with sickle cell disease over the age of thirty years and publication of the work in 1968 changed concepts of the disease. For the first time it was realized that doctors may not see older patients with sickle cell disease because they had improved with age.

Dr Sergeant realized that the patients seen in hospital were a biased group so he needed to do follow-up studies of them among less biased patients. As a result, Sickle Cell Clinics were started in the following hospitals: Morant bay, Annotto Bay, St Ann's Bay, Mandeville, Montego Bay and Black River, the last three still operate so patients do not have to travel to Kingston.

A lot of information was secured about the complications, treatment and natural history, which changed international thinking on sickle cell disease. The big question for Dr Sergeant now was: if someone with the sickle cell disease could die within the first year of life or be compatible with survival to age 78 years, why is the disease so variable? It was obvious that if other genetic and environmental factors modified the disease, identification of these factors may give important leads in the understanding and treatment of the disease. This led Dr Sergeant to the Sickle Cell Cohort Study.

The cohort study involved 100,000 normal deliveries at the Victoria Jubilee Hospital in Kingston between 1973 and 1981. This study detected 550 children with all genotypes of sickle cell disease who, along with 250 normal children, are followed in special cohort clinics. Over five thousand patients are followed islandwide. The Jamaican Cohort Study is recognized worldwide as a major contribution to the understanding and improved management of sickle cell disease. For the first time, the true pattern of a disease in the community was being studied and not just the affected patients attending hospitals.

Indeed, the experience gained from Sergeant's work in the organization of clinical services for sickle cell disease and of clinical research over the last 43 years in Jamaica has proved invaluable in advising and assisting on the development of sickle cell services in other developing countries.

In 1999 Dr Sergeant was conferred Professor Emeritus, Faculty of Medical Sciences, UWI, Kingston. Among his many awards are: Special Gold Musgrave medal from the IOJ for contribution to medical science (1995); Pelican Award of the UWI Guild of Graduates (1995); Vice Chancellor's Award for Excellence (1999); Humanitarian Award by the Sickle Cell and Thalassemia Patients' Network, New York (2004).

# Professor Owen Morgan - Medicine

Professor Owen Morgan of the University of the West Indies, Mona Campus in Kingston, was elevated to the distinguished rank of Mastership of the American College of Physicians at the College's annual ceremony held in April 2006 in Philadelphia, US. This seminal honour is granted to only a small group of highly distinguished Fellows of the College, who have achieved outstanding recognition in medicine. This was a milestone in the history of medicine in the West Indies.

Morgan is professor of medicine and neurology and emeritus dean of the Faculty of Medical Sciences, Mona. He also holds an endowed chair, named in his honour, the Owen Morgan/Paul Dishner Chair in Medicine, a first in the history of the University of the West Indies.

In his citation, the college identified Professor Morgan as the epitome of the outstanding clinician-educator-investigator who instituted new graduate training programmes, and served as a member of the advisory committee which recommended the formation of the Regional Caribbean Accreditation Body for medical schools. His fundamental and important research contributions were in the field of human retrovirology and its associated neurological diseases. As a consequence of this research, he has served as consultant on retroviral diseases to the World Health Organization (WHO). He is also credited with more than 100 publications in international peer-reviewed journals.

# Dr Augustus Grant – Medicine

Cardiologist Dr Augustus Grant became president of the American Heart Association (AHA) in 2003, making him the first Jamaican cardiologist to head America's largest organization dedicated to fighting cardiovascular disease.

Grant, professor of medicine and co-director of the heart station, joined the Duke University faculty in 1980. Since securing an AHA grant in 1974 to support graduate research at the University of California at San Francisco, Grant has been active within the organization by receiving grants and organizing scientific sessions.

Dr Grant, whose research and clinical efforts are focussed on better understanding and treating cardiac arrhythmia, had as his major goal during his presidency the advancement of the association's goal of reducing the incidence of heart attack and stroke by 25 percent by 2010 thorough patient education. He said: 'We have developed many expensive technologies for testing heart disease, and while these have saved many lives, patients have an important role to play by leading healthier lives. The AHA can play a crucial role in educating patients about the control they have in preventing heart disease and stroke.'

The American Heart Association is the largest non-profit health organization fighting heart disease, stroke and other cardiovascular diseases, which annually kill about one million Americans.

# Dr Roger Hunter - Medicine

Neurosurgeon and chief resident at the University Hospital of the West Indies, Dr Roger Hunter, received in 2006 the prestigious Braakman Diploma and prize by the European Association of Neurosurgical Societies (EANS). Dr Ivor Crandon, head of the department of neurosurgery at the university hospital said: 'This is a unique achievement for both Dr Hunter and the University of the West Indies. Dr Hunter is the first Caribbean citizen to have won the Braakman prize.'

After leaving Jamaica College, he enrolled at the University of the West Indies, choosing medicine and then neurosurgery as his specialty, graduating in 1996 with the bachelor of medicine, bachelor of surgery (MBBS) degree with honours. He won most of the subject prizes that year.

He previously sat the primary examination (part one) of the European Association of Neurosurgical Societies (EANS) in Uppsala Sweden in February 2005 and was top in the UK and second overall. In March 2006 he received the award for being the best candidate at the oral part two examination of the EANS examination in neurosurgery.

Hunter tied with Martin Schumman of Leipzig, Germany, who along with him, was subjected to a third sound of orals in order to determine who would come out on top. Hunter came out on top. The Braakman prize is named after a Dutch neurosurgeon who sought to harmonize neurosurgery training throughout Europe.

The best candidate in the oral examination is awarded the Braakaman Diploma/Prize. With this award, Dr Hunter could, in the near future, choose to work in any country in the world. As a neurosurgeon, he will treat such conditions as brain aneurysms which can lead to massive haemorrhages, brain tumours, cancers of the brain and spinal tumours.

# DR WAYNE BATCHELOR – MEDICINE

Dr Batchelor migrated to Canada in 1966. His dream was to be a doctor who specialized in cardiology and he achieved that dream in Canada. He received the highest distinction in his undergraduate studies. He became an Interventional Cardiologist and was co–director of clinical trials in Interventional Cardiology at the Terrence Donnelly Heart Centre, St Michael's Hospital in Toronto.

Dr Batchelor was also an Assistant Professor of Medicine at the University of Toronto. Up to 2002 he was the only Black Interventional Cardiologist in Canada. Dr Batchelor is the author of over 50 published articles on cardiology, has written several book chapters in Interventional Cardiology textbooks and divides his time between research and regular contribution to the American Journal of Cardiology and the Journal of American Cardiology.

Dr Batchelor is a member of the American College of Cardiology, The Canadian Cardiovascular Society and the Association of Black Cardiologists. He has received many academic honours and awards including: Dean's Award for Excellence in Clinical Research, Junior Research Fellowship Award, Heart and Stroke Foundation.

# Professor Renn Holness – Medicine

Dr Renn Holness arrived in Canada in 1972 and worked his way up to the position of Director of Surgical Education in the department of surgery at Dalhousie University. Since 1977, he is the Staff Neurosurgeon at the now – Queen Elizabeth II Health Sciences Centre. In 1992, he became the first neurosurgeon in Canada to perform fetal tissue transplants for Parkinson's disease.

On several occasions he has been a guest lecturer at Morehouse Medical School in Georgia. He has demonstrated his great interest in medical education in developing countries by regularly returning to the Caribbean to carry out surgery and to assist in the training and the examination of medical students and neurological trainers.

Professor Holness was a member and President of the Canadian Neurosurgical Society; member of the Editorial Board, Canadian Journal of Neurological Sciences. He has also received many honours including: Distinguished Service Award, 2000; UWI 50th Anniversary Alumni Achievement Award, 1998; Distinguished Graduate Award, UWI, 1996.

# AINSWORTH ALLEN - MEDICINE

Ainsworth Allen left Titchfield High School in Portland, Jamaica with 10 'O' levels under his belt, a barrel pickney who was brought up by his grandmother. He went to New York to join his mother, Millicent James. He was enrolled in New York City High School but because his aptitude surpassed every other child at New York City High, he was asked to leave at 2 ½ months in the first semester. He later registered at New York Queens College. During the summer months, he registered for the summer programme at Harvard University. Four years later at 19, he graduated with a BSc in Chemistry.

His grandmother, Lena Irving, instilled in him that he could do anything, there was no barrier as to what he could do or accomplish. Today, he is one of the leading Orthopaedic surgeons in the United States. After graduating from Queens College in 1982, he chose Cornell University where he received a full scholarship and admission into their medical school. There, he worked with one of the world's renowned researchers, Dr Steven Arnoczky. The only set back was that as a first year student he was not supposed to operate. However, because Dr Arnoczky was doing a lot of research in sports medicine, ligament and cartilage healing, he kept asking his tutor to change the rules. The Jamaican's determination made history and changed the culture, rules and regulations of the institution in seven months.

After graduation, his next feat took 130 years to become a reality in the United States. Dr Allen went back to New York and joined the staff at the Hospital for Special Surgery (HSS) as one of the first Black surgeons to work in such an institution.

# MUSIC

# Shirley Thompson

She is often described as one of the most original and gifted composers in contemporary Britain and she always tries to incorporate the myriad of influences in her work, which makes her a reflection of the multicultural environment of which she is a part. Thompson has researched and directed documentary films in addition to her many musical achievements.

This daughter of Jamaican parents was raised in Newham in East London. Even though this is one of the most ethnically diverse sections of London, in the early 1960s it was almost culturally monolithic. This forced her to be aware of identity at an early age.

After leading the Newham Youth Symphony Orchestra from age 17, Thompson studied music at Liverpool University, where her skills as a composer were recognized. She returned to London and completed her master's degree at Goldsmith's College. There, she studied under South African composer Stanley Glasser who stimulated further diversity in her work.

Very soon after her graduation, Thompson was commissioned by the Arts Council to write a piece for the 1985 Greenwich Festival. The piece 'Visions' was performed at the Royal Festival Hall.

In 1988, Thompson composed the award-winning soundtrack *Dreaming Rivers* a film by St Lucian director Martine Attille. The following year, her themes to the popular BBC television series *South of the Border* also won an award.

Returning to the work of complex compositions, she formed the Shirley Thompson ensemble in 1994 and her opera, *A Child of Jago* won her the woman of the year award in Britain in 1997.

In 2001, Thompson received the rare honour of an invitation to perform at Buckingham Palace. She also impressed the Queen with her violin playing at the Commonwealth Day celebrations. The following year, she was commissioned to write the music to accompany the Queen's official visit to East London, which led to the commissioning of her symphony *New Nation Rising* based on Newham's vibrant thousand-year history.

# Sir Willard White

Willard White with over 50 roles to his credit and a Grammy award winner, was in 2004 highly regarded as the world's greatest baritone singer. In 2005 the Queen of England awarded White a Knighthood. Famous for his rich bass voice and powerful stage presence, White has performed in some of the greatest opera houses of the world accompanied by many of the world's most celebrated orchestras.

His extraordinary voice was discovered while he was a student at Excelsior High School in Kingston. He first studied music at the Jamaica School of Music and later was admitted to the renowned Julliard School in New York. It was not long before he was appearing with the New York City Opera and then it was on to the United Kingdom where he continued to excel, singing a range of challenging roles with premier opera companies.

In 1995 he was made a commander of the order of the British Empire (CBE) and in that same year his Silver Musgrave Medal was upgraded to Gold Medal for distinguished eminence in the field of music.

Sir Willard White has since delivered first class operatic music to audiences in countries such as Great Britain, France, Czechoslovakia, Spain, Norway, Canada, Australia and Israel.

# CLIVE CAMPBELL (DJ KOOL HERC)

DJ Kool Herc was not a star in Jamaica, but he was a follower of the popular DJs, and he played a major role in the evolution of rap and hip-hop just by leaving Jamaica. He moved to New York in the late 1960s, secured a sound system, and started using it at block parties in the Bronx and in New York style, entertained the party goers by deejaying over the pulsating sounds.

So what was to become rap in the late 1970s into hip–hop, originated two decades earlier in the dance halls of Jamaica. As such, Herc may be described as the first hip–hop DJ and he played a pivotal influence on Grandmaster Flash, who was to become rap's first serious hit-maker in the mid-1970s.

This cross–pollination has continued with Jamaican artists like Sean Paul and Shaggy emerging from the island's dancehall scene to attain international recognition, and being featured on compilation albums along with today's generation of hip–hop superstars.

Hip–hop and rap join an already long list of the English-speaking Caribbean's remarkable contributions to popular culture, along with ska, rock steady, calypso, soca, reggae, the steel pan, rapso, mobile sound systems, dual–turntable mixing, and the greatest musician of the 20th or any other century – Bob Marley.

# Bob Marley

There is a vibrant movement for Bob Marley to be made a national hero in Jamaica. When he died, his vision of one world, one love was beginning to be listened to worldwide and the last tour in 1980 before his death attracted the largest audiences at that time for any musical act in Europe. His legacy of songs is like a reference book for the oppressed throughout the world. As such, his work transcended all categories, classes and creeds.

Bob was undoubtedly the first superstar from the Third World with a music that originated in the street culture of Jamaica. Bob was born at Rhoden Hall in St Ann to 18 year–old Cedella Booker and Captain Norval Marley, a 50 year–old white quartermaster attached to the British West India Regiment.

Bob and his mother moved to Kingston when he was a teenager and settled in Trench Town. Although he tried welding for a while, music was his passion and he linked up with Bunny Livingston in order to pursue that passion. He auditioned for a local music entrepreneur, Leslie Kong, who was quite impressed by the quality of Bob's vocals. A few tracks were cut. His next move was to join the Clement – Sir Coxsone – Dodd who had a studio and also one of the finest sound systems in the country. Bob had also linked up Neville Livingston known as Bunny, with whom Bob took his first step in music. The first single, 'Simmer Down' shot to number one on the charts and caused a sensation. Later Bob and Bunny met Peter McIntosh and together they formed 'The Wailing Wailers'.

Bob then met Rita Anderson and married her. He was later drawn into Rastafarianism as the movement got more popular. This led to a split with Coxsone Dodd. The Wailing Wailers formed their own label but because of business ignorance the label folded. However, they continued to write songs and formed an association with American singer Johnny Nash who had an international recording success with Marley's 'Stir It Up'. Later the 'Wailers' joined up with Lee Perry a music production and recording studios genius. They produced quite a few hits that defined the future of Reggae Music.

While stranded in London Bob and the Wailers signed up with Island Records which was owned by Chris Blackwell. This deal offered Marley and his group the best recording facilities and they made the album 'Catch–a–Fire'. It broke through on the international market and became a big seller.

After a club tour in the UK, they went on an American tour which played to packed houses and a weekend engagement playing support to the young Bruce Springsteen. It went so well that a tour was arranged with Sly and the Family Stone, then the top black band in America. After four shows, the Wailers were taken off the bill. They did too well; the crowd supported them more than the main band, it seemed.

'Exodus' was released in 1977 and established the band's international status. The album remained on the UK charts for 56 straight weeks, and three of its singles were massive sellers.

After the One Love Peace Concert in 1978 in Jamaica, he was invited to the United Nations in New York to receive the medal of peace. At the end of the year he visited Africa for the first time, going to Kenya then Ethiopia. Then in 1980, the band was invited by the government of Zimbabwe to play at the country's independence ceremony. This underlined the Wailers' importance in the third world.

The band then went on a major European tour which included a 100,000-capacity crowd in Milan, Italy, the biggest show in the band's history. At the end of the European tour Marley and the band went to the US where Bob performed at two shows at Madison Square Garden but immediately afterwards, was taken seriously ill. A toe that was injured while playing football became cancerous.  The cancer had spread to his stomach, lung and brain and he died in 1981. Before he died, he received Jamaica's Order of Merit, the nation's third highest honour.

# HARRY BELAFONTE

Fame follows Jamaican singer, actor and political activist, Harry Belafonte wherever he goes. He grew up in the US but never forgot his strong Jamaican roots which put him in the news with the 'Banana Boat Song', the album 'Calypso' which was the first album to sell a million copies and 'Carmen Jones,' the iconic film he made with Dorothy Dandridge. He made the headlines again in 1985 when he brought together America's top 45 artists to record 'We are the World'. Recently, in 2006, he made the news for calling the President of the US, George W. Bush, the 'world's greatest terrorist' and Colin Powell, Secretary of State, a 'house slave'.

He returned to Jamaica occasionally to visit his cousin, Veronica Dumont, one of his few living relatives at the family home in Aboukir, a village in St Ann. Belafonte is constantly in the news because he asked powerful and pertinent questions, which caused people in the African Diaspora to think. A recent question is how useful was it to have Colin Powell and Condileeza Rice in the White House?

This Jamaican is one of the greatest networkers in recent history. Belafonte is linked with many, if not all, of the black men and women who have made history in the second half of the 20th century. In May 2006, he was in Jamaica as guest speaker at a dinner to honour Dudley Thompson who made history by having defended Jomo Kenyatta at his trial in Kenya for his alleged involvement in the Mau Mau rebellion.

How, what, where did he get the motivation and influence to accomplish all that he did? He read widely and always had mentors – Dr W.E. Dubios, Paul Robeson and Eleanor Rosevelt. As such, he has always been deeply involved in class issues and class struggles. Belafonte summed it up: 'There is no question that a certain kind of political and social bent is deeply rooted in my Jamaican/West Indian character and roots. My mother was a feisty woman from St Ann. She would never accept indignity. She instilled in her children to never compromise with the oppressor. Never think that there was anything we couldn't achieve or attain – even in the face of enormous crisis. My mother didn't even finish elementary school in Jamaica, and had no opportunity for too much education in America. But I think that the lack of formal encounter, that formal experience should not be permitted to diminish people's capacity for genius, the capacity for courage and the capacity for analysis. Some of the greatest people of our time could not read or write.'

Belafonte is aware that these are serious problems of low self-esteem amongst blacks in the Diaspora mainly because of that lack of knowledge of self, so he advised the leaders of the future: 'We must get away from the sense that we have no potency, are somehow neutered, impotent, if we didn't have all the bourgeois trappings of life. This is not true'.

Regarding the tragedies in Africa and Africans in the Diaspora tending to be invisible toward each other he had this to say: 'We have got to stop looking at our lives inside the box. We have a propensity for that. Whether our oppressors designed it that way, we do not really see each other.'

'We need to know in detail who we are, how we evolved, how we got here…but moving forward is the key. I wake up every morning having wiped out of my mind any sense of capitulation. I do not see momentary defeat as permanent. I wake up with another opportunity to look at the chessboard and to see where the enemy has moved his pieces and determine how I move mine.'

# Soweto Kinch

Soweto Kinch, born in London to Jamaican actress Yvonne Harris with roots in Lucea, is a Saxophonist and rapper who has been described as one of the most exciting musical talents to emerge in Britain in recent years. He won the 2003 Mercury Prize for his debut composition 'Conversations With the Unseen.' Soweto has also toured internationally, composed for stage plays, acted in a movie and collaborated with South African dramatists.

Although he was born in London, he grew up in Handsworth in Birmingham. His father is the celebrated Barbadian playwright Don Kinch. Encouraged by his artistically oriented parents and community, he had been playing the alto sax since age nine.

How did he get started? At a cultural centre in the African–Caribbean community they had open days where people could try out different instruments and he saw someone playing a shiny saxophone in a room and thought that was what he wanted to do.

A major turning point in his life was at age thirteen, Soweto met trumpeter Wynton Marsalis one of the world's best known jazz musicians. He went to his performance then sneaked backstage and rather than kicking him out, Marsalis rapped with him for nearly two hours explaining what jazz meant to him. Marsalis was enthused and moved that a young teenager was showing an interest in jazz. From that moment, it was the pursuit of the jazz heritage and getting to grips with the roots of the music that absorbed young Soweto.

# GRACE CARTER–HENRY LYON

Grace left Jamaica for Canada in 1973. In no time she established herself as the founder and Musical Director of the Heritage Singers in 1977. Its aims were to promote the development of Caribbean folk music and theatre; use music and dance as tools to bridge cultural gaps internationally; enhance ethnic, historic and social traditions; and, to share the heritage with the larger community.

Since its inception, the group has performed in a number of international locations, including Jamaica, the US, the Netherlands, Taiwan, Germany and Mexico; produced recordings and videos; and been the subject of a CBC documentary. Partial proceeds from their performances have been given to charitable organizations. Grace has also worked in Real Estate and received many awards to mark her success.

Her community involvement includes: Jamaican Cultural Committee; the Arts and Culture Committee; Metropolitan Toronto Community Folk Arts Council; Maple Downs Investment.

She has received many honours including: Harry Jerome Award, for Excellence in Business; Woman of Excellence Award, Congress of Black Women, 2000; Several Awards in Real Estate.

# NURSING

# Couba Cornwallis

Without this little known Jamaican woman, Couba Cornwallis, Horatio Nelson might not have gone on to fight the battle of Trafalgar. Horatio Nelson is regarded as one of England's greatest naval heroes, who owed the last 25 of his 47 years of life to this black Jamaican nurse and healer in the tradition of African herbal medicine.

Nelson, at the time was stationed at Port Royal as a young officer in the British Navy and took part in an expedition against Fort San Juan de Nicaragua in the Gulf of Mexico. The expedition was a disaster. Many were killed and Nelson himself suffered from dysentery and high fever.

On his return to Port Royal, he was so weak that he had to be taken ashore on a cot and carried to the lodging house and nursing home of Cornwallis. There, she nursed and cared for him, administering drinks of herbal mixtures and bathing him in pans of hot water seeped with various weeds and leaves. Today, we would call this a 'bush bath'.

Nelson recovered to continue his naval career, latterly defeating a combined French and Spanish fleet at what has since become known as the 'Battle of Trafalgar'. He was killed in the battle, and an open space in London was named Trafalgar Square in his honour. In Jamaica, there is a plaque mounted on the wall of Fort Charles at Port Royal on which is inscribed: 'In this place dwelt Horatio Nelson, you who tread his footprints remember his glory'.

Couba Cornwallis also nursed Prince William, Duke of Carover, when he fell ill while visiting Port Royal as a midshipman. He too was cured. He later became King of England and as a thank you gift, his wife, Queen Adelaide, sent her a costly and elaborate gown in appreciation of her services.

# MARY SEACOLE

Mary Seacole is undoubtedly Jamaica's most famous nurse. She was born Mary Grant in 1805 in Kingston and was destined to become the heroine of the Crimean War. Her mother was also a healer and ran a boarding house for the recovering officers.

She was well educated and a skilled nurse. When the Crimean War broke out in 1836 she travelled to London and applied to go to the Crimea, the peninsula which extends from the South of the Ukraine into the Black Sea, to tend to the wounded soldiers, but she was not granted an interview by the British War Office. She then applied to Elizabeth Herbert, the wife of the Secretary of State for War, who was recruiting nurses for the war effort, but was again denied an interview. After some time, she received a rejection letter. Britain apparently, was not ready to welcome a black nurse.

Mary did not give up. She travelled on her own initiative and in 1856 established the British Hotel near Balaclava, a valley in the Crimea, using her own money in order to provide a 'mess table' and comfortable quarters for sick and convalescent officers. Mary spent many hours on the battlefield attending the wounded.

After the war ended Mary was left with several unpaid debts that caused her to go bankrupt, but her story was carried by the British press and money was raised by subscription to pay off her debts.

In 1857, she published *The Wonderful Adventures of Mrs Seacole in Many Lands*. The book was a great success and Mary Seacole became a popular figure. She spent the rest of her life travelling and working between London and Kingston. She was awarded the Crimean Medal, the French Legion of Honour and a Turkish medal. Mary Seacole died in 1881.

# Daphne Bailey

Ever since Mary Seacole, world famous Jamaican nurse, left the shores of Jamaica for England then on to Sebastopol to establish Jamaica's fame in the nursing profession, many have followed in her footsteps. Daphne Bailey has been one such follower. She went to England too, after completing her nursing studies, both as a State Registered Nurse and a State Certified Midwife. She migrated to Canada in 1960 and worked at the Brentford General Hospital and at the Doctor's Hospital. Later on, she joined the Victoria Order of Nurses as a community Health Nurse.

While at the Victorian Order, she helped develop tools for the evaluation of nurses; was an early discharge nurse for mothers and babies and later worked in the areas of footcare and as an infusion specialist, taught healthy aging to seniors. Today, she is the owner of D&B Footcare Business.

Her other community involvement include: member of the JCA since 1963; the North York Seniors HC; the Advisory Committee on Seniors' Issues for over six years, giving input to various levels of government.

She has received various honours including Award for Volunteerism.

# Professor Enid Collins

Enid Collins started her nursing career in Jamaica before migrating to Canada in 1961. On her retirement in 2001, she had been teaching nursing for over 30 years in Canada. Her first position in Canada was an obstetrical nurse at the Royal Victoria Hospital in Montreal, where she worked with immigrant women. The women's limited knowledge of the language and the system in which they found themselves increased her awareness of the impact of culture shock and led her to become an advocate for this group.

After two years, she enrolled at McGill University and completed studies in Public Health and Nursing Education. She later completed graduate degrees in Nursing, as well as Sociology and Equity in Education. In 1969 she began teaching at the Hospital for Sick Children School of Nursing, where there were no Black nursing students and no other Black instructors. In 1973, she went on to teach at Ryerson School of Nursing, and remained there until her retirement in 2001. During her tenure she served as a mentor and role model, particularly to students and colleagues from minority groups who usually suffer racial discrimination.

Her research interests have included investigation of Nurses' complaints related to workplace discrimination. She continues to conduct research on career mobility among immigrant women in nursing. Among the honours she received include: Professor Emeritus, Ryerson University, 2001; Race and Ethnic Leadership Award, North York City Council, 1997. She has published in Health and Cultures and Holistic Education.

# Politics and Public Service

# Colin Powell

In the 1920s Luther Powell left Top Hill in Saint Elizabeth for America. Colin Powell's mother, Ariel, left around the same time for America. Luther and Ariel met in New York City, and Colin was born in 1937. His parents constantly stressed the importance of education and personal achievement. However, although he listened to his parents, when he left high school in the South Bronx, where he grew up, he had no idea as to what he wanted to become.

He entered the City College of New York to study Geology and it was there that he found his 'calling' when he joined the Reserve Officers Training Corps (ROTC). Powell became commander of his unit's precision drill team and graduated at the top of his ROTC class, with the rank of Cadet Colonel, the highest rank in the corps.

Later, Powell was commissioned a Second Lieutenant in the U.S. Army, and was one of sixteen thousand military advisors dispatched to South Vietnam by President Kennedy in 1962. In 1963, Powell was wounded while patrolling the Vietnamese border with Laos. On his second tour of duty in 1968-69 he was again injured in a helicopter crash. Although injured, he managed to rescue his colleagues from the burning helicopter. Powell was awarded the soldier's medal. In all, he has received 11 military decorations, including the Legion of Merit.

On his return to America, he earned his MBA at George Washington University in Washington DC, and after being promoted to Major, won a White House fellowship. During the administration of President Nixon, he made a lasting impression on the Director and Deputy Director of the Office of Management and Budget: Casper Weinberger and Frank Carlucci.

Powell was later promoted to the rank of Colonel. He followed his term in the White House with service in Korea as a battalion commander then a staff job in the Pentagon. He later served as assistant commander and deputy commander of infantry divisions in Colorado and Kansas before returning to Washington as senior military assistant to secretary of defense Casper Weinberger.

In 1986 Powell became deputy to Frank Carlucci, after Carlucci was appointed Secretary of Defense and Powell became the Assistant to the President for National Security Affairs. In 1991, as Chairman of the Joint Chiefs of Staff (Army, Airforce and Navy) under President George H.W. Bush, Powell became a national figure during the successful Desert Shield and Desert Storm operations which pushed the Iraqi army from Kuwait.

In 2001, the newly elected President George W. Bush appointed Colin Powell as Secretary of State which up to that time was the highest rank ever held by an African American in the US government.

# Whit Stennett

Whit Stennett's life demonstrates that you can lift yourself up from any type of situation. At the age of 13 he had a defining moment in life when he was struck by lightning. He survived the incident and it helped him to overcome his fears. Whit described his youth as that of an angry young man. The anger was felt as a result of the frustrations encountered with the social and political conditions in pre-independence Jamaica. He was full of ambition but the opportunities were few and far between.

Whit left Jamaica for England in 1959 to take up an opportunity in Manchester, trial to play county cricket. However, he went into politics instead and later became the first Black Mayor of Trafford. On his journey, he experimented with different routes to his destination including Communism, Rastafarianism, Garveyism and Christianity. Because of the contradictions in all of them, he took from what was beneficial to him and discarded the rest.

Some high points on his journey were: member of the Order of the British Empire in 1998, his degree from Manchester Metropolitan University in 2002 and, of course, becoming Mayor of Trafford in 2003. In 2008, he also received the Governor General's award for Jamaicans in the Diaspora.

The story of Whit Stennett's life is recorded in his autobiography entitled *A Bittersweet Journey* which was published in 2007.

# Boukman

Desperation and the will to be free fuelled the Tacky rebellion in 1760. This rebellion dwarfed the maroon wars and was an islandwide conspiracy, which lasted six months. The aims of the leaders included driving out the white population and partitioning Jamaica into principalities in the tradition of the Akan-speaking Koromanti who were at the heart of the rebellion.

One of the leaders, a man called Boukman, fled to Haiti when the rebellion was finally crushed. There, in Haiti, he ignited a struggle for freedom, which ended with the expulsion of the last foreign soldiers from Haitian soil (John Maxwell in Sunday Observer, August 22, 2004, in an article entitled 'The Anti-Boukman League').

'Bwa Kayiman' celebrates the occasion on August 14, 1791, when the Jamaican escaped slave Boukman, presided at a meeting to plan the rebellion against the French. At a place called Bwa Kayiman – Crocodile Forest – delegates from all over the north of Haiti pledged to throw off their chains and throw the French out of Haiti forever. Boukman is said to have invoked the God of the Africans, who he said '… takes us by the arm and guides us. He will give us assistance. Throw away the white God's image. Who is thirsting for the water in our eyes! Listen to the call of freedom in our hearts!'

The delegates returned to their plantations. On D-Day, August 22, 1791, the orders discussed and adopted on the night of August 14 were implemented, thus started the great saga that culminated in the independence of the first black nation in the hemisphere. Boukman was killed November 1791 in a French counter-offensive. His severed head was exposed with this caption: 'Head of Boukman, the rebel leader'.

There is some controversy about whether Boukman was a voodoo priest/obeahman, or a literate Moslem. John Maxwell (Sunday Observer, August 22, 2004, in 'The Anti-Boukman League' reported that in a monograph, Max Manigat said: 'It has been said that he had been given the name "Book Man", as was the custom in the English colonies of the Caribbean, in the case of many slaves who knew how to read the Koran'.

# DIANE ABBOTT – POLITICIAN

Diane Abbott was born to Jamaican parents in London, England. Diane is a member of the British Labour Party in parliament, representing the Hackney North and Stoke Newington constituency. In 1987, she became the first Black woman to be elected to the House of Commons and remained the only black female Member of Parliament for ten years until she was joined in the Commons by Oona King in 1997. In 2008, she was named one of the most powerful black women in Britain by Powerlist magazine.

Dianne went to Harrow County Grammar School for Girls and then to Newham College, Cambridge where she read history. After university she became a fast-tracked civil servant, later working as a Race Relations Officer at the National Council for Civil Liberties. There, she met Harriet Harman, Patricia Hewitt and Paul Boateng, all later became Labour Party cabinet minister rank members of Parliament.

Soon after being elected to office, Abbott unsuccessfully attempted to establish a Black caucus within the Labour Party along with Bernie Grant. She tried again in 1989 but was still unsuccessful as senior Black MPs argued that it was fundamentally racist to create a 'party within a party.'

Abbott was also involved in community politics including, Organisation of Women of African Descent (OWAAD); the 'Scrap Sus' campaign to ban police stop-and-search tactics leveled at black youth, and was a founding member of the Black Media Workers' Organisation.

# Alvin Curling

He was born in Jamaica and actually worked in the management of housing and land settlement before immigrating to Canada. In 1985 he became the first Liberal Member of Parliament elected to the riding of Scarborough North. In his first win in 1985, he recorded the highest total vote in Canadian history, and has since been re-elected four times, making him one of the longest serving members in the Ontario Legislature.

In 2003, he retained his seat and was later voted Speaker by MPs on both sides of the house, becoming the first Black Canadian and the first Jamaican to hold the prestigious position. That same year as part of its 46th anniversary celebrations, the University of Technology chose to honour Curling by making him the third inductee into the institution's Hall of Fame.

As a boy in Franklyn Town, Curling joined the youth club, the local boy scout groups and various sport teams, activities which allowed his leadership potential to develop and shine. It was that easygoing and firm leadership quality which took him through school in Jamaica, and after leaving CAST/UTECH to migrate to Canada, it propelled him to leadership positions at Seneca College where he became President of the Students' Council.

Recently, he was named as Canada's Ambassador to the Dominican Republic.

# MARY ANN CHAMBERS

She was born in Vineyard Town but grew up in a comfortable home in the outskirts of Kingston. She was one of four children of a homemaker and an airline executive. Chambers emerged as a natural leader at both prep and high schools. However, her parents were quite disappointed when she sidelined a career in medicine for one in the then little known world of computer programming and marriage to a systems analyst, whom she met during a short stay at IBM.

The couple left for Canada in 1976 and Chambers was hired by Scotiabank within days of their arrival. She started out as a computer programs/analyst then after completing her degree in 1988 with a major in commerce, she moved quickly up the corporate ladder to become senior vice president of electronic banking services.

At age 54 she entered representational politics. Though new to the field of politics, in 2003, she trounced the Tory incumbent who had held the Scarborough east riding seat since 1995 by more than 6,000 votes. When the new Premier Dalton McGuinty put his cabinet together, Chambers was named Minister of Training, Colleges and Universities. The political neophyte is now in charge of post–secondary education, overseeing apprenticeship programs as well as the province's 18 public universities and 24 community colleges. So, from motivating staff at Scotiabank, where she began in international systems and rose to vice-president in charge of electronic banking, to her extensive volunteer efforts with a myriad of community organizations across Toronto, Chambers has always looked out for others. She said 'I was introduced to volunteerism by my mother through her activities with the church and was also introduced to looking after others who were not as fortunate as I was. In elementary school I used to go with the nuns into some of the poorer areas in Kingston to teach reading to kids who didn't attend school. I loved it and found it fulfilling.'

# YVETTE CLARKE

Yvette Clarke of Jamaican parentage was elected representative of the 40th district in Brooklyn to the New York City Council – a post previously held by her pioneering mother former city council member, Una Clarke. Yvette, a descendant of the Maroons said: 'I am very big on family. My parents instilled that in us from an early age. I was born in the United States but I have been coming to Jamaica since I was a baby. My mother was adamant that we be aware of where we came from.'

Clarke has a strong background in public policy development and got a public policy fellowship in 1985 to study at State University of New York at Stonybrook. There she did intensive research on current theories that drove government agencies, non-profit organizations and the private sector and what made them responsive to social issues. That same year she returned to work as a child care specialist/family day care coordinator at Erasmus Neighbourhood Federation.

In 1988 Clarke became executive assistant to Assembly woman, Barbara Clarke of Queens. This stint gave her hands-on experience in working with legislative sub-committees and caucuses. Clarke became an expert in understanding the relationships between the legislative process, the local concerns and the legislative responsibility of lawmakers.

Clarke is a highly motivated individual. Her strength and motivation she said comes from knowing her roots: 'As a black person in the US you still have to deal with racist elements but if you are rooted you can deal with persons as equal. My family is a strong one, we are rooted in the maroons who were a strong and courageous people. They survived slavery and their courage inspire me.'

# MARCUS GARVEY

When Marcus Garvey returned from the United States in December 1927, the crowd that welcomed him home was the largest single gathering ever witnessed in Jamaica. The hero of the moment was a deportee who had spent just over two years in a federal prison in Atlanta, Georgia for a dubious misdemeanor.

Marcus was born an uncompromising advocate for the transformation of the condition of black people worldwide. That was his real crime. Both white America and the ruling class in Colonial Jamaica saw that as dangerous.

Some years before, after travelling to Latin America and England and witnessing first-hand the living conditions of black people, he founded the Universal Negro Improvement Association (UNIA). When he migrated to New York in 1916, the UNIA became a mass organization – one of the largest membership organizations in the world.

The blacks Garvey found in the US desperately needed a leader. There was a growing contradiction within the society – blacks in the north were making some progress but felt excluded. Those in the south were experiencing increased social violence and deepening segregation.

Blacks who had served in World War 1 and who had returned expecting to find respect and acknowledgement, were extremely disappointed. It was into this leadership vacuum that Marcus Garvey, the mesmerizing orator and tireless organizer, came. He provided a leadership that was militant and assertive. His leadership threw cold water on the spineless 'hat-in-hand' image of the black man and emphasized black pride, black self-reliance and international black unity.

It was not surprising that within a few years Garvey had established 727 chapters and divisions of the UNIA throughout the US and boasted a membership of 750,000 people. Indeed, at a UNIA convention at Madison Square Garden, New York, in 1920, some 25,000 members were present.

At its peak, Garvey's newspaper, *The Negro World* had a worldwide circulation of 200,000. Garvey had made a fantastic impact on the world in 1920.

# Karlene Leiba-Davis - Health

Karlene was educated at Titchfield High School in Portland and later trained as a nurse and mid-wife in Nottingham, England to where she had migrated in 1967. The daughter of Inez and Herman Leiba, was recognized in 2001 for her many years of service and sterling contribution to Britain's National Health Service and to developing the practice of midwifery in the United Kingdom when she was awarded one of the highest national honours in Britain after being appointed Dame Commander of the British Empire in the then Queen's honours list.

Her achievements include working at the Regional Health Authority in the United Kingdom on policy as well as managing the educational budget for nurses and midwives. She was deputy, then general secretary of the Royal College of Midwives, which campaigned for regulation of the profession.

In November 2008, Karlene was recognized by the University of the West Indies with an honorary doctorate for her contribution to health.

# Dr Rosemary Brown

Dr Brown left Jamaica for Canada in 1951 where she studied social work and worked in that area. She later gained distinction of being the first black woman in Canada to be elected to public office in 1972 in British Columbia, serving as a member of the provincial legislature until 1986. She is also the first black female in Canada to run for the leadership of a female political party 1975, finishing, after four ballots, a very close second in the New Democratic Party (NDP) leadership race.

After completing her studies, Brown worked with the children's Aid Society of Vancouver, the Riverview Mental Hospital, the Montreal Children's Hospital and as a Counsellor at Simon Fraser University (SFU). In 1987, she was the Ruth Wynn Woodford Professor of the Endowed Chair in Women's Studies at SFU, is a former CEO of MATCH International and continues in the role of President of the NGO which works with women in developing countries. She has participated in many national and international conferences on peace, women's issues and human rights. In 1993, she was appointed Chief Commissioner of the Ontario Human Rights Commission and served until 1996. Dr Brown has also received many honours which include some 15 honorary degrees from universities across Canada. She is a recipient of the Order of Canada; Order of British Columbia, Order of Distinction, Jamaica and Member, Privy Council.

# DENISE CAMPBELL

Denise Campbell migrated to Canada in 1980. In 1999 she became the first Young Feminist Vice President of National Action Committee Status of Women (NAC), Canada's largest feminist organization and created the Young Women Network when she took office. Then, in 2001, at age 26, she became the youngest president of NAC; she had been active in the community for many years as a youth activist and community organizer. She has travelled extensively as a motivational speaker, addressing issues of racism, women, and youth empowerment and has appeared on local and national media and was featured in educational videos on volunteerism, child poverty, etc.

Campbell often represented a youth perspective for various media, including CBC TV and radio, YTV, Much Music. In 1996, she co–hosted Girl Talk on WTN for ten episodes, and co–produced an educational video on gender issues with young women; she has also hosted a six part series on international development, 'Global Villagers,' and since worked on an eight–part follow–up on globalization.

Campbell has also participated in a number of global conferences including: the G-7 and People's Summits, 1995; the UNESCO conference on the Environment and Education in Greece, 1997; co–created Challenge the Assumptions!, a multimedia educational package on systemic gender issues with 150 young women from 10 countries; participated in UNWCAR in South Africa with a two year project working with young women to explore the barriers they face at the intersection of race and gender.

Campbell has received several honours including Young Woman of Distinction, YWCA; Harry Jerome Award, Youth; Youth Achievement Award, YTV; GG 125TH Anniversary Medal; Lincoln Alexander Anti–Racism Award.

# RELIGION

# MONSIGNOR GLADSTONE WILSON

Roman Catholic priest, Monsignor Gladstone Wilson, was born in 1905 and was hailed in his lifetime as the seventh most learned man in the world, stated Michael Burke in the *Daily Observer*, Thursday February 7, 2008 in an article entitled 'Things we do not like to hear'. At age 23, he achieved the first of three doctorates.

Born in Mavis Bank, St Andrew, of parents that were both school teachers, Wilson was tutored privately before going to high school. His parents attempted to get him into Jamaica College, which had at least one black student among the mostly white student population at the time who was a famous schoolboy athlete. But since the young Wilson did not have the land–class background of the black skinned J.C. athlete, he was refused entry.

As a result, Wilson was enrolled at St George's College and by age 15, he knew more about the subjects than the subject teachers at St George's, stated Michael Burke, Jamaica Observer columnist in The Daily Observer, Thursday March 10, 2005. On leaving school, Wilson entered the Civil Service at a time when only the brightest graduates of Jamaica's high schools could be employed there. He later entered the Urban College in Rome where he received a bachelor's degree after only one year and winning the Latin, Greek, Natural History awards and the Chancellor's Philosophy Scholarship.

Wilson was so bright that he was ordained before time by special permission in 1931. He was the only Caribbean national at the time that was on the faculty at the Urban College, where he lectured in philosophy. Indeed Pope Pius XI personally congratulated him for a speech made at the 50th anniversary of the Urban College in 1929.

Gladstone Wilson, who was a candidate for the Vatican Diplomatic Service, spoke 14 languages, seven in which he was fluent. These included most European languages, but also included Chinese. In fact, during the Second World War, there were German and Italian prisoners of war here, and he was the official interpreter.

# Dr Oliver Lyseight – Religion

Dr Oliver Lyseight migrated to the United Kingdom in 1953 and settled in Wolverhampton. A devoted Christian, he started attending the Methodist Church but it was not long before he started to experience racism.

Dr Lyseight started to explore the area for a church home in order to preach the gospel. In his meetings with other persons of colour he discovered that they too were experiencing the same racism. Indeed, some were so fed up with the insults that they stopped going to church. As such, Dr Lyseight was determined to start a church where fellow brethren could worship in a comfortable way. He started with prayer meetings in homes then found a hall in the YMCA building. The pastoral development came under the umbrella of the New Testament Church of God which is active in both Jamaica and England. As the news spread, the congregation grew. Branches were established in Birmingham, Walsall and London and Dr Lyseight was made National Overseer by the State Board in the USA.

Dr Lyseight continued to tour the UK preaching the gospel, while his wife Rose led a group of singers who accompanied him on the tours. It did not take long for the church to become established and accepted in British society. Under Dr Lyseight's watch, the church expanded throughout the UK. Today, the New Testament Church of God has over 107 branches and over 10,000 members.

# Dr Pat Francis

Shortly after Pat Francis reached Canada she got involved in various women's ministry groups. In one of the meetings the speaker could not make it so she preached. On many occasions after that she was asked to preach. Then, while holding down a job as a radiographer in a Canadian hospital, she found herself travelling to speaking engagements overseas.

She started a Friday evening bible study in her home with ten persons. This grew rapidly. After a while those who she was teaching asked her to become their pastor. Without any formal teaching she moved headlong into ministry. Eleven years later, she has a staff of 30 which includes seven pastors who help to give care to the more than 3000 persons representing about 70 cultures who attend services on the weekend. Moreover, her church operates more than 100 programmes designed to assist in the care of souls and the transformation of society.

Her church conducts regular programmes dealing with such matters as wealth creation, managing money, getting out of debt and earning money from the government.

So successful have these teachings been that in 2004, 120 of her members bought their own homes. Dr Francis is herself the president of several for profit companies. These include a call centre, financial services company, and a recording company. She is also president and founder of four charities.

She grew up in the Mountain View area of Kingston and went to Alpha Academy before moving on to the University of the West Indies where she graduated after studying radiography. Though starting out in pastoral ministry without formal theological qualifications, she now holds two Master's degrees and a Doctoral Degree from the Christian School of Theology, Columbus, Georgia in the USA.

# Reverend Owen Burey

Reverend Owen Burey migrated to Canada in 1966. He later became the pastor of the Sandwich First Baptist Church in Windsor, Ontario, a church built by former slaves following their arrival in Canada via the Underground Railroad. The church was built in the 1840s then rebuilt in 1851. This church is one of the oldest churches in the Windsor area and now part of the African Canadian Heritage Tour.

Revd Burey who has been a pastor since 1986, is also a teacher by training and has worked in the correctional services. In 1992, he became a Chaplain, coordinating pastoral services for the Ministry of Community and Social Services, Southwestern Regional Centre.

His community involvement include: Vice President, National Council of Jamaicans in Canada; Moderator, Amherstburg Baptist Church; Board of St Josephs Hospital; International Services Canadian Red Cross Society; Kent County Task Force Committee on Family Violence; Children's Aid Society; Volunteer Probation Officer.

He has received honours including: Volunteer Award, Government of Ontario, 1995 and 2000; Volunteer Award, Government of Canada.

# Reverend Rose Hudson-Wilkin

Rose Hudson-Wilkin, Anglican Priest and Vicar at Holy Trinity, Dalston and All Saints, Haggerston in the London diocese, describes herself as 'a mother of three children and one husband!' She was born and grew up in Montego Bay, Jamaica. She was attached to the St Francis Mission in Glendevon. St James where she was trained in the Church Army before moving to the West Midlands in England in 1979. Her theological training was at the Queens Theological College in the West Midlands. She also gained a Bachelor of Philosophy in Education from Birmingham University.

For Hudson-Wilkin, it was not an easy road to become a female priest She recalled coming up against conservative male attitudes in the church after her marriage and the birth of her first child. When she tried to pursue ordination, the authorities were basically dismissive. Then, the law changed in 1994 in her favour and she broke new ground, becoming one of the first women to be ordained as a priest.

She later became Vicar at Holy Trinity, Dalston and all Saints, Haggerston in the Diocese of London. When she took over the church in Haggerston in 1998, it was facing redundancy – on the verge of closing its doors since only a handful of members remained. She did not believe that the spirit of God had left the community. Her first task was to renew the grounds and the building and, over the years, the congregation started to grow again. Today, nearly 300 people celebrate and worship there on Sundays.

Then, in early 2008, she was invited to be one of 36 religious leaders who were invited to officiate and preach on occasions at the 400 year-old Queen's Chapel beside St James' Palace in London. As such, she is the first Black Chaplain to the Queen of England.

# Road Builder

# CLAUDE BELL

Claude Bell was born in the district of Retreat in the parish of St Mary in 1890. As a young boy he went to Titchfield High School in Portland, later joining the British army and served in World War I including a tour of duty in Egypt. Whilst in Egypt, he saw and marveled at the wonder and grandeur of the pyramids, Sphinx and the awesome river Nile.

The work in Egypt was very hard. Being a desert and very dry, all the water came from the great river Nile. In the army, he learned about various tools and machinery used to build roads, houses, and waterways to get water from the river.

When he returned to Jamaica, he brought back a lot of problem-solving skills which could be applied to the myriad of problems in Jamaica at the time. In 1938 the people were uneasy because they wanted more jobs, better pay and living conditions. Claude Bell was asked to help and he had just the plan. There was a great swamp called Tinson Pen which covered acres of lands which were not in use. He asked to transform the swamp into dry land. Hardly anyone believed he would succeed. He reminded them quite rightly that there had been swamps on the airport road and it was he who cleared them to allow the good road to be built just before the onset of World War II. Thousands of people were employed by the project and he made use of the shift system so that everyone would earn some money. It was not unusual for the workers to find crabs, shrimps and wild ducks which they ate.

It was not long before the land was drained to produce dry land. A wide road called Foreshore Road was built, bordering the dry land. It was linked to three miles where Spanish Town Road meets Hagley Park Road. This road was later renamed Marcus Garvey Drive.

Claude Bell was not just good at draining away water, he was also good at finding it. In fact, he also went to other countries to make use of his skills. Today, Bell Road is named in his honour.

# SCIENTISTS

# Dr Mark Harris

Dr Mark Harris, a geoscientist, completed research that he believed can stop the corrosion of zinc roofing by red mud waste from bauxite mining operations, a recurring source of discontent between bauxite firms and people living in mining areas.

According to Dr Harris, a geoscientist at Northern Caribbean University, gypsum, a limestone material, in combination with young decomposed leaves from the Poinciana plant, can do the trick of neutralizing the corrosive effects of red mud dust.

Clay, Dr Harris said, is treated with caustic soda or sodium hydroxide in order to dislodge aluminum from microscopic soil particles during the bauxite production process. However, the caustic soda treatment leaves high salt or sodium residue in the red mud dust which, when transported by wind, attacks metal surfaces such as zinc coated roofing.

However, in laboratory experiments done in collaboration with Dr Pichu Pengasamy of the School of Earth and Environmental Sciences at the University of Adelaide, Dr Harris found that gypsum curtailed the adverse effects of sodium in soil, such as bauxite red mud wastes.

The findings were published in *Environmental Geography*, the international journal of geosciences, which has previously published studies done by Harris and his colleagues.

Subsequent to the initial experiment focusing on the use of gypsum, the NCU faculty member has done follow-up laboratory experiments in Jamaica which revealed that crushed leaves from the Poinciana tree, when applied to red mud over a nine-month period, caused a more pronounced reduction in alkalinity of the bauxite waste, a role not performed by gypsum.

In addition, the NCU researcher stated that the detoxification of red mud would prevent the contamination of ground water sources, thus making water safer to the consuming public.

# Professor Anthony Chen

Prof. Chen, formerly Professor of Physics at the University of the West Indies (UWI), Mona was lead author on the work of the Intergovernmental Panel on Climate Change (IPCC), which last year (2007) shared the Nobel Peace Prize with former United States Vice President, Al Gore.

Professor Chen, Dr Leonard Nurse, Lecturer in Coastal Management at UWI Cave Hill and Dr John Agard, senior lecturer in Life Sciences at UWI St Augustine, contributed to the research on climate change, which won the IPCC prize 'for its efforts to build up and disseminate greater knowledge about man-made climate change and lay the foundations for the measures that are needed to counteract such change.'

A startling conclusion from the study is that persons in developed countries have a one in 1,500 chance of being affected in a natural disaster, while in a developing country the probability is one in nineteen.

# GLENN C. CHIN

Chin was born in Kingston, Jamaica, and moved to South Florida in September 1979. He graduated from the University of Miami with a Bachelors of Science Degree in Mechanical Engineering. He is a National Aeronautics and Space Administration (NASA) mission manager in the Inter-nation Space Station and Spacecraft Processing Directorate at the John F. Kennedy Space Centre in Florida.

His primary responsibility is to lead the multi-disciplinary team of engineers and technicians that assemble and test the inter-nation Space Station components that fly aboard the space shuttle. Additionally, he is the primary customer advocate and the primary payload interface to NASA launch vehicle management and international space station programme management.

Chin joined NASA in 1989 as a systems engineer working in the 'hands-on' assembly, integration and test group that processed space lab modules and experiments for the space lab programme. In 1992, he moved on to being a payload project/integration engineer for the space lab programme where his primary role was technical requirements and test management. He was awarded the NASA exceptional service medal in 2005 and a silver snoopy award in 1995.

# Professor John-Paul Clarke

The US Department of Transportation's Federal Aviation Administration (FAA) presents an award yearly to individuals or institutions whose contributions through research in aviation have significantly improved the national airspace system. Through this award, the FAA formally recognizes the value of aviation-related research efforts. In 2003 the FAA made the award to Professor John-Paul Clarke of the Massachusettes Institute of Technology's Department of Aeronautics and Astronautics.

Professor Clarke, a Jamaican, is recognized globally for his contribution to noise and emissions modelling and simulations.

His specific accomplishments include:

- Developing a unique three-dimensional noise simulation and design tool that factored in atmospheric conditions
- Creating a new method for noise abatement procedures; forming and leading the research team that designed and flight-tested a noise abatement procedure that reduced community noise
- Developing a system for assessing global emissions

Prior to joining the MIT Faculty, Professor Clarke was a visiting scholar at the Boeing Company and a researcher at NASA's Jet Propulsion Laboratory.

He is the son of Jamaicans, Canon the Rev. Dr Gervais Clarke, an internationally known track and field official and his wife, Dr Joan Binger-Clarke, formerly of the Bustamante Children's Hospital in Kingston Jamaica.

# Professor Bertram Fraser-Reid

Professor Fraser-Reid's career development from youth to adulthood is a source of inspiration to many. He was born in 1934 in Jamaica where he pursued his education to secondary level. After leaving High School – Clarendon College – he developed an interest in chemistry and practically taught himself the subject, with the help of the book *Read Yourself Chemistry*.

He credits his success to discipline and a quest for excellence. His father taught at Bryce Elementary School where he was the headmaster and where Prof. Fraser-Reid spent the first nine years of his life. They never had a radio or a gramophone but there were lots of books and he would read them at nights. He strongly believes that it was that early introduction to reading that opened the door to the wider world.

At age 12 he began his secondary education at Excelsior High School in Kingston where he developed a love for music. He would skip school and go to concerts and as a result came second to last in his class. His father took him away and sent him to Clarendon College where he spent four years. The tutors at the college were not well prepared to teach the sciences and Fraser-Reid found physics beyond comprehension.

One day, he went to Sangster's Book Store and bought a book entitled: *Teach Yourself Chemistry*. He read it and decided that it was what he wanted to do. So, in 1956, at age 22, he enrolled at Queen's University in Canada and pursued his Bachelor's and Master's degrees in Chemistry. Later, he went on to the University of Alberta in Canada where he did his doctorate in Chemistry. He studied the use of nuclear resonance in determining the structure of complex molecules.

Professor Fraser-Reid worked in a post-doctoral position at the Imperial College in London, England, where he was exposed to international chemistry. This exposure equipped him with the necessary experience to conduct similar research projects of his own. In his many research activities, Professor Fraser-Reid discovered that sugar could be used to create carbon-based chemicals, medicines, plastics and paints. He also discovered that sugar cane and beet derivatives could be used in the chemical industry as a raw material, rather than petroleum. This research offered alternatives for the production of plastics and also presented options for the energy sector.

By the 1990s he had published over 250 papers and had visited 42 countries as an invited lecturer at Scientific Symposia. Over the years he has received many awards especially in the field of chemistry which includes the award in Carbohydrate Chemistry (1990), Haworth Memorial Medal and Lectureship of the Royal Society of Chemistry, United Kingdom's World Premiere Award in Carbohydrate Chemistry and the recent Gold Musgrave award and many nominations including that of the Nobel Prize award in Chemistry in 1998.

# Dr T.P. Lecky

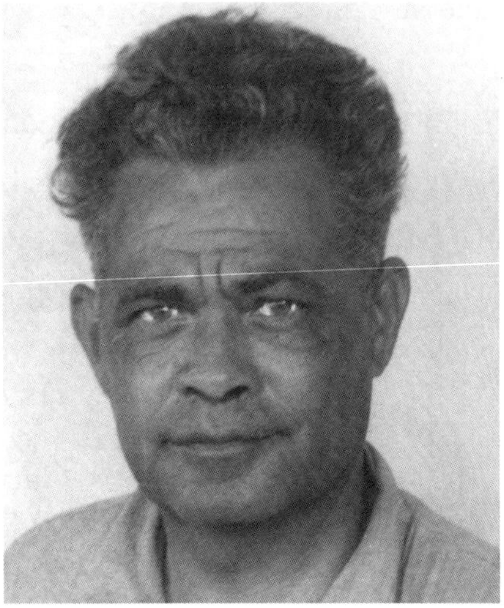

Thomas Phillip Lecky was born on a small farm to parents Andrew and Margaret Lecky on December 31, 1904 at Swift River in Portland. Thomas was very bright and he won a merit scholarship to the new Farm School at Hope Gardens in St Andrew.

Lecky did well at the Farm School especially in Agronomy, animal husbandry, farm sanitation, accounts, land surveying and other subjects. His passion was for animal husbandry and he decided that he would dedicate the rest of his life to ensuring that small farmers in Jamaica were able to have an animal development on their farm, no matter how small. His major problem, however, was how to get small farmers in Jamaica to own cattle when the cattle which existed were not suited to small, hillside farms.

At the time, most Jamaican cattle were direct descendants from animals brought by the Spaniards in the 16th century, mixed with cattle brought from India by the British, and bred for strength and size. The Indian cattle, the ZEBU, were white, had huge curved horns, and a massive hump just behind the neck, and had a low proportion of meat to bone in their bodies. Although immensely strong and with low resistance to several tropical diseases, the milk produced was barely enough to sustain their calves.

To assist him with his monumental task, he studied Agriculture at McGill University and the University of Toronto. Lecky decided that by studying genetics, he would discover the best animal for the Jamaican small farmer.

Lecky came up with a method which produced dramatic results in less than 20 years. The cows were now producing an average of 15 quarts of milk daily and were resistant to tick fever and could withstand drought, high temperatures and a variable diet.

In the 1950s, Lecky presented the outline of his plan to develop a dairy breed for the Tropics. These were accepted by the University of Edinburgh, where he was awarded the Ph.D. He became the first Jamaican to gain a doctorate in Agriculture.

At Bodles in 1952 he presented the first examples of the new breed he had developed and named it the Jamaica Hope – one of the world's first scientifically engineered breeds of tropical cattle. At that time, most Jamaican cattle produced about four litres of milk daily, but the Jamaica Hope could produce an average of 12 litres daily, and some of the best animals gave 30 litres per day. It was indeed a revolution in tropical farming, and scientific and government officials from all over the world came to Jamaica to find out how Dr Lecky achieved it. He went on to develop other breeds of cattle suited to Jamaica.

# Dr Karen Nelson

Dr Karen Nelson, an Immaculate Conception High School past student, is a microbiologist who is working to spell out the entire genetic code of different microbes at The Institute for Genomic Research(TIGR) in Rockville, Maryland, USA. She led the research team that came up with the whole genetic sequence for a bacterium called Thermotoga Maritima which lives in very hot water.

She describes herself as someone who is interested in microbial physiology – the study of chemical reactions in microorganisms and environmental microbiology, the study of microbes in the environment. She then links the two through genomics, the study of living things' DNA.

Dr Nelson had an interest in science at an early age. When she was at prep school in Jamaica she always had a curiosity about how things worked. She went in the science stream at High School to further her interests. A great love for animals was developed and she initially wanted to be a veterinarian. However, when she was exposed to ruminant microbiology, which is the study of the roles that bacteria and fungi played in the guts of ruminants - a technical word for animals like cows – she realized that she had a passion for microbiology. After she graduated with her Masters' degree in Animal Sciences from the University of Florida, she went on and completed the Ph.D. in Microbiology from Cornell University. TIGR took her on and the rest is history.

Her advice to others: 'I believe that when we are kids and we think we can only be doctors or lawyers we are not really aware of all the many options there are out there. I would encourage kids to be curious and explore as many of these avenues that come their way and they will find something they do enjoy'.

# AUSTIN JAMES THOMAS

He was born in Westmoreland in 1909. Austin was a self-taught scientist who became an international consultant. Jamaica, although an island, was almost totally dependent on imported fish especially the fresh water fish. Austin's passion was to do something about it.

Thomas was the government fisheries officer in 1949, and he was sent overseas to find a species of perch that was suited to Jamaican conditions. In Africa, he found the perch as ideal and returned to Jamaica set on adapting it to our use. He built ponds and began to nurture the perch. The first fish, the tilapia mossambica, were not popular with local housewives, even though they were tasty.

However, most of the fish did not develop and remained very small. Thomas, undaunted, soon discovered that the male fish, reared together by themselves grew fastest. A system of sex selection was developed and only male fish were allowed to thrive. The 'monosex culture' was being used on perch for the first time. This monumental achievement has led to a billion dollar industry in countries as far apart as Israel, USA and Jamaica.

In 1978, the silver perch variety was introduced and it became an instant success amongst the housewives. The success of the programme led the Food and Agricultural Organization (FAO) to hire him as a consultant, and he was sent to several parts of Africa to assist in getting an improved diet for the local people.

Thomas' great achievement was to mechanize Jamaican fishing operations and develop a system for breeding the African Perch commercially. He sincerely believed that Jamaica could produce enough pond fish to meet all its protein needs. This was all developed at Twickenham Park in St Catherine. Today, this fish is one of the most widely bred and produced in the world.

# Dr Howard Reid & Dr Russell Steele

Today, tilapia is the third largest imported aquaculture product entering the US following just behind farm-raised shrimp and Atlantic salmon. The dream of Dr Howard Reid and Dr Russell Steele is to complete the creation of a multi-million dollar industry growing tilapia fish in sea-water – as against the customary fresh water pond.

A study into the island's aquaculture industry that was conducted in 1993 by the FAO, which gave great relevance to the work of the two scientists stated quite clearly that unlike countries such as Costa Rica and Guyana, Jamaica did not have sufficient bodies of fresh water to sustain an aquaculture industry.

It was therefore recommended that the island should set about studying marine cage culture with respect to marine species.

Steele started the research into the rearing of tilapia in sea water over twenty years ago as the then professor in the Department of Life Sciences at the UWI and continues to make his considerable experience available to the Mona Institute of Applied Sciences (MIAS) which took over some years ago.

Head of MIAS, Dr Howard Reid, said: 'once we have completed the pilot projects, we have several options. We can get a venture capital partner or contract farmers to whom we license the technology and have the UWI earn from that'.

The fish had been acclimatized to growth in salt water, through cages at sea and via inland tanks. The team of researchers had also been able to handle the troublesome parasite that has been known to blind or even kill the tilapia. Indeed, there was also a higher meat to bone ratio in sea water–grown tilapia and its taste could be equated to that of the snapper but 'with more meat'.

# PROFESSOR GEOFF PALMER

Geoff Palmer's mother migrated to the UK in 1948 leaving him to be reared by his aunt until his mother was ready to send for him. He left Jamaica in 1955 to join his mother and to finish his schooling. At Shelton Road Secondary in the middle of London, there were not even black people on the streets much less in the school. In his school he was the only black child.

Palmer should have left school early in England but because of his love and skill at cricket he was given a scholarship at a grammar school. When he left grammar school, because of his race, he was unable to find a job. Palmer took refuge in the library and read widely. One day he saw an advertisement for a job as a technician at London University. He applied and got the job. A professor there helped him to get into the University of Leicester. He gained a bachelor's degree in Botany then returned to London. No one would employ a black man with a degree in Botany so he secured a job peeling potatoes in a restaurant.

He saw an advertisement for a doctorate in Edinburgh, applied for it and got it. He received his doctorate in 1968 and secured a job with the Brewers Research Institute and became a senior scientist. He later went to Heriot–Watt University in Scotland as a lecturer where he has remained since. Professor Palmer made several forays into Africa to consult and teach about the brewing industry. It was much cheaper for him to go there and teach 20 students than for 20 students to go to Edinburgh to be taught.

During his research period at the research institute in Scotland where he worked on barley, he made a scientific discovery which earned him worldwide recognition. Professor Palmer said: 'with barley, it is made into malt which is used in the making of whiskey, milkshakes, beers, ovaltine, Milo, bread and other products. With my experience in barley my job was to make malt most efficiently; so in 1970 I developed a process where you could make malt in five days instead of nine days which was the norm in those days.'

His greatest concern was that when he retired there would not be another senior professor in that university who is black. He believed that there was a greater awareness among black nationals of what they want to be – at the top.

# DR FRANKLYN PRENDERGAST

In 2004 Dr Franklyn Prendergast, an outstanding Jamaican scientist, living in the US, was awarded the coveted Musgrave Medal. This son of Linstead and a past student of Calabar won a Rhodes scholarship and studied at Oxford University. He later became a well-respected researcher and director of the Mayo Clinic comprehensive cancer research in Rochester, Minnesota.

Professor Prendergast is one of the top 50 earners of grants from the national institution of health, USA. He has published over 150 research papers based on findings from research in the dynamics and function of proteins, the biochemistry and biophysics of bioluminescence, bio imaging and computational biology.

Dr Prendergast's career path is decorated with numerous awards and accomplishments. He graduated with honours from the University of the West Indies in 1968 then went to Oxford in1969 as a Rhodes Scholar. On his graduation from Oxford with a Bachelor of Arts and Masters Degree in Physiology, Dr Prendergast subsequently completed a Ph.D. in Biochemistry at the University of Minnesota.

His extensive involvement in numerous professional organizations and societies in the United States included the National Academy of Sciences, the National Cancer Advisory Board and the American Chemical Society.

The Musgrave Gold Medal is awarded for distinguished eminence in Literature, Science or Art.

# PROFESSOR JONATHAN FARLEY

In 2004, Professor Jonathan Farley who is considered young, bright and an authority on mathematics was the recipient of the Harvard Foundation's Distinguished Scientist Award in recognition of outstanding achievements and contributions in the field of mathematics. The son of a Jamaican mother, Professor Ena Farley, a former Regent for the state of New York, the young Farley co-founded the phoenix mathematical systems modeling.

As chief scientist for his company, Phoenix Mathematics, he and his partners Dr Stefan Schmidt and Lennox Farwell have developed mathematical and software tools to help with counter terrorism and to anticipate trends in the stock market. He is also a co-founder of Hollywood Math and Science Film Consulting, which offers advice for movies that have a math or science element.

Professor Farley said that many other institutions examine social, political, public policy and bioterrorism issues, but that none looks at the mathematical analysis of counter terrorism. His theory for using math for academic and economic growth is perhaps superseded by that of his alternative approach in examining homeland security issues.

Farley explained that, 'It's not enough to disconnect terrorist networks. A remnant may yet contain a leader and enough followers to mount serious attacks. My method uses the order theory to analyze their effectiveness, and to quantify the degree to which a terrorist network is still able to function.'

Professor Farley's work that applies the order theory to counter–terrorism analysis and breaking Alqaeda cells, was recently profiled in the chronicle of higher education and science news online. As an example of the power of mathematical theory, which he also applies, to understanding trends on the stock market, Farley and his partner Dr Stefan Schmidt have put their reflexive theory to the test. They used US$5,000 and watch it multiply to US$45,000.

In recognition of his many outstanding accomplishments, the city of Cambridge, Massachusetts declared March 19, 2004 'Dr Jonathan Farley day.'

# Dr Kevin Fenton

Dr Kevin Fenton, as a youngster, had dreams of being a pilot. However as an adult he settled for a career in medicine. Because of his work, research and publications, he was placed in 2005 at the top at the renowned Centers for Disease Control and Prevention (CDC) in Atlanta, Georgia, USA, a pivotal organization in international public health.

Through his father, Sydney Fenton, Dr Fenton said he learned to appreciate the value of knowledge. As a result, he believed in an education that went beyond books, so over time he developed interests in fine foods, music, travelling, languages and painting. In medical school he received several honours and medals, and was voted class president (1985-86) and Vice President of the UWI Medical Students Association (1987).

In 1992, he secured a Carreras Post Graduate Scholarship to pursue a masters in public health at the London School of Hygiene and Tropical Medicine. He got on very well with the faculty members whose passion for the subject rubbed off on him.

In the United Kingdom, after completing his masters, Fenton worked in the field of clinical infectious diseases for 18 months, after which he was appointed a lecturer in HIV/AIDS epidemiology, and was made honorary specialist registrar in public health medicine at the medical research centre.

In addition, he was the first chair of the English Chlamydia screening programme and was a co-investigator on the second British National Survey of Sexual Attitudes and lifestyles. With his research, he has authored and co–authored several works in his field, the latest of which was published in 2005, *Reported Sexually Transmitted Infections in Britain: Prevalence, Risk factors, and Proportionate Burden* by Fenton and nine others.

# DR HENRY LOWE

Henry Lowe and Nigerian Dr Ajibike Salako–Akande developed an alternative nutritional supplement to fight drug addiction, working with psychosocial support - mentoring, counseling etc. A crucial part of any effective substance abuse programme, this revolutionary approach product gave overwhelmingly positive results after extensive research was done in the United States.

Dr Lowe pointed out that the use of substitution drug, such as methadone, to control addiction was limited in scope and potential and often produced side-effects. He added that persons across various social and professional strata who are battling addiction to heroin, cocaine, marijuana, tobacco, alcohol and even prescription drugs would rather not exhibit these side effects.

A pharmaceutical chemist by training, Dr Lowe assisted with the formulation of the nutritional supplement under the brand 'Bio–recovery' while Dr Slako–Akande was the lead US researcher in charge of the clinical work in Baltimore. The later test proved the new approach to be highly effective. The supplements are in capsule form and contain amino acids and micro nutrients. Different dosage levels have been formulated for different types of drug addiction and they were found to be over 90 percent effective in the management of drug addiction. The internationally accepted recovery, based on conventional treatment is somewhere between 20 and 30 percent.

# Leonard Lewis

In 2004, Jamaican-born Leonard Lewis, who lives in the USA brought home the Cumsee ointment to the attention of the public. The ointment is a derivative from the annatto plant. He developed the drug that originally served as a cure for sores and used as remedies for arthritis.

Lewis is from the district of Cumsee in St Mary, from where the ointment got its name. He studied for four years at West Indies College, now Northern Caribbean University, before going to Michigan University for graduate studies. He has since increased the product line by adding the oil of annatto.

After introducing the lotion to residents in St Ann, people experienced the miraculous results and word spread to other parishes. Indeed, persons with sores deemed untreatable were cured. At least one medical officer, District medical officer for St Ann, Dr Arthur Green, has recommended the product for use after seeing the results on sores ten years old.

Dr Green said: 'I have seen at least two persons, females, who have had chronic leg ulcers, large ulcers on the legs for well over five to ten years, that means they have been through the mill – clinic, doctors, everywhere getting treatment with limited response, meaning that up to the point when I saw them the ulcers were still unhealed. 'Having being exposed to this product and since it is an external product, I recommended it to two of these patients and personally I have seen marked improvement in less than six weeks. In other words, we saw that there was reduction in the size of ulcers, there was increase in the granulation – the reforming of the skin and, in one lady in particular, hers completely healed over.' Dr Arthur said the product has been tested and used successfully in hospitals in America and Jamaica.

# Dr Carl Blackwood

Dr Carl Blackwood was born in the parish of St Elizabeth to parents who were headmaster and teacher. He was nurtured in a home environment where education and the pursuit of sound values were uppermost. Those values were to take him and guide him in the pursuit of knowledge and higher learning in Trinidad, France, England and the USA where he eventually made significant discoveries and inventions that made a mark on the world.

In 1965 Carl left for St Augustine in Trinidad to study engineering. His stay in Trinidad brought to the fore his deeply ingrained values on social justice rather than the study of engineering. He was passionate about the divisions between the Blacks and Indian population. Carl got mixed up in Trinidadian social politics and was eventually jailed.

He was later released and tried to return to Jamaica to see his father who had taken ill. He left Trinidad for Jamaica and was declared 'persona non grata' as soon as the aircraft left Trinidad airspace. He arrived in Jamaica under strict security surveillance and lived under security watch when he resided with his parents in Harbour View.

He applied for and received a new passport with the change of government in 1972 and subsequently applied to every embassy for a travel visa, but was refused by all except the French embassy. Carl was told he could travel freely to Paris and there seek permission for a more permanent status from the relevant authorities. In Paris, he was warmly welcomed and met a wide range of African freedom fighters, and other leaders, who were engaged in struggles for justice in their respective countries.

Having resided in France for more than a year and a half, he discovered, quite by chance, that as a French resident he was eligible to study in England. After many deliberations with the British consulate in Paris, he was allowed to continue his engineering studies in Britain. He eventually settled on the University of Hull in East Yorkshire, which had an excellent reputation for its work in Electronic Engineering and Applied Physics. He registered at Hull for a special honours degree in Electronic Engineering.

His brilliance was rewarded by coming first in controls group, his chosen specialty, in the BSc Engineering Special Honours degree. At the same time he also did his Diploma in Engineering which thesis was deemed to be of such high standard that he was allowed to bypass the masters degree course and proceeded directly to the

Ph.D. degree. He was given a full scholarship to read for his Ph.D. His dissertation entitled: 'Robust Identifiers for A Class of Adaptive systems' was cutting edge in its day.

His dissertation was considered to be brilliant and he graduated to a standing ovation with prolonged applause as he received the letters for his degree from the late Lord Wilberforce the grandson of the late British Slave Abolitionist Movement, Sir William Wilberforce.

He was sought after by job offers from five countries including the USA, Britain and Sweden. He applied to Jamaica but there was no job available. He received offers from two universities in the USA but had to be cleared by British Security.

He was warmly welcomed in the USA as he arrived to take up his professor's job at a prestigious university Lehigh University in Bethlehem, Pennsylvania. In one year his performance surpassed all expectations in research, teaching and consulting. He was adequately rewarded for his efforts. His research was of strategic value then and his inventions addressed some fundamental shortfalls in the defense of his adopted country.

Carl later started his own company, but he was then persuaded by an offer he could not reasonably refuse to lead a large research effort at a major aerospace company in California's Silicon Valley.

He invented many cutting edge technologies and systems for de–icing planes, and sheer detection devises to prevent air disasters, and systems for detecting land mines. He developed some of the early algorithms for GPS navigation and altitude determination, and worked on re-entry systems. He also developed the first KA–band RF autotrack systems for geostationary satellites, and was once given the freedom to be his own one-man think-tank for one year with all the support and resources he required.

At present, he is developing the means for greater spacecraft autonomy, far surpassing some of the most sophisticated spacecraft currently in orbit. One of his last large programs, built for the Japanese, is currently in the ninth year of its expected sixteen-year life. The expectation is that this mark will eventually be far exceeded. Carl is also working on Novel Adaptive Neural Network control schemes for large space platforms.

# PROFESSOR LOUIS GRANT

Professor Louis Grant was born in Clarendon to a family with a proud and strong scientific tradition. His father Henry Grant was among the first black men to manage a sugar estate and credited with developing the famous Appleton Rum in the chemistry laboratory at the Appleton Estate.

At primary school his brilliance shone and he won a scholarship to Jamaica College. From Jamaica College where he received his high school education, Louis Grant went to the University of Edinburgh, then the London School of Tropical Medicine and Hygiene where he specialized in microbiology. He enjoyed the pursuit of knowledge and eventually secured seven academic degrees.

It was not long before he was called on to make use of his vast research knowledge. In 1949 Tuberculosis was rampant in Jamaica. He was successful in his approach to the World Health Organization (WHO) and the United Nations Children's Fund (UNICEF) and secured a significant grant to start a campaign of inoculation against tuberculosis in Jamaican children. The team was headed by Dr Grant and Dr Ronald Lampart and as a result the incidence of tuberculosis in Jamaica was significantly reduced by the 1950s.

Grant was rewarded for his brilliance in 1964 when he became one of his first Jamaicans to be made a full professor at the University of the West Indies, Mona. Not long after, another disease reared its head. This time it was among the horse population in eastern Jamaica. His laboratory work soon revealed that it was a virus that had invaded Jamaica. His measures for containment were successful and the lucrative horse industry was saved by Grant.

Professor Grant was also credited with identifying the dengue fever from which Jamaicans were suffering in the 1960s. He recommended measures which managed and prevented further growth or spread. Further research into dengue virus led to establishment of arbo–virus as a major research topic at the UWI. These viruses were affecting the population in a serious way. He later discovered a particular strain of influenza found only in Jamaica. This discovery earned him further international acclaim.

The pioneering work of Louis Grant earned him the title of Jamaica's father of microbiology. His legacy was a highly trained team of microbiologist that gave Jamaica a highly respected name in this area of science.

# Dr Albert Lockhart and Dr Manley West

While on a visit to El Salvador in 1972, Dr Albert Lockhart learnt of the intro–ocular pressure lowering effect of ganja smoking. On his return to Jamaica, he contacted his friend and colleague Dr Manley WeSt Dr West by this time was hearing from fishermen that their night vision was greatly improved by ganja smoking. They decided to investigate and that was how a very productive research partnership started.

When they started their work, they co-opted Dr Henry Lowe but Dr Lowe left in the very early stages before they could arrive at a process for the production of any medical extracts. After much research at which they paid for themselves, West and Lockhart have produced a number of active ingredients.

> **Canasol**: The original extract is used in the treatment of glaucoma. Not only has the drug changed the way glaucoma is treated, but it has revolutionized the entire treatment of glaucoma. However, the most important factor is that Canasol does not have any adverse effects on patients unlike the other glaucoma drugs.
>
> **Asmasol**: This extract is used in the treatment of asthma and respiratory congestion. It is unique in that it has no ephedrine or blood pressure, and it does not produce drowsiness. In its unusual or slightly modified form, it is used in patients or treatments for cancer as it reduces vomiting, nausea and appetite.
>
> **Canivert**: This extract is on trial now for motion sickness. It differs from other medications for motion sickness in that it does not affect vision or glaucoma and it does not cause dry mouth or drowsiness.
>
> **Cantimol**: This is a combination of Canasol and Timolol for the treatment of glaucoma. It acts much faster and longer than either by itself and the concentration of Timolol is much reduced thereby reducing the side effects of Timolol.

West and Lockhart who were trained at prestigious academies in England, Scotland and the United States were both awarded Jamaica's highest medical honours: the Order of Merit for Medicine and the Musgrave Gold Medal.

# Dr Paula Tennant

Jamaican Papaya farmers were making good money from export of the fruit. However, ever so often a new disease would enter the island and devastate the crops. During one such event, a young Paula Tennant secured a summer job in the Botany laboratory at UWI Mona Campus. She had completed the teacher's diploma at Shortwood Training College. Tennant had a passion for science and decided to pursue a degree in biology at UWI. A new papaya disease broke out just as she entered the lab to start her summer job.

A consultant from Cornell University came to Jamaica and recommended a procedure /system to deal with the disease but after a while he realized that the problem was more complex than he had thought. The discussions were fascinating to Paula to the extent that she decided to study Botany instead of Biology. She enjoyed the course and graduated with first class honours and was selected to visit Cornell and work in the laboratory where the Jamaican papaya virus was being investigated.

Paula laboured until she identified the virus. She went further and manipulated the genetic material in the cells of selected papaya plants and produced a new strain. As such, she became the first person in the Caribbean to produce / develop a bio – engineered product. After several experiments, she developed many variations to meet the different requirements of the farmers and consumers. Her efforts earned her the Ph.D. from Cornell and special recommendations from Dr Dennis Gonsalves, then one of the world's leading authorities on papaya plant.

# Dr Barrington Batchelor

Barry Batchelor had a passion for civil engineering. He went off to England and studied it, returned to Jamaica where he practiced for a while. Barry worked as a Senior Executive Engineer then branched out into his own engineering firm and was the principal in Franks and Batchelor, Consulting Engineers.

Dr Batchelor migrated to Canada in 1966 where he took up a post at Queen's University lecturing in Civil Engineering. He soon became an associate professor, then Chairman, School of Graduate Studies and Research. Batchelor later became Professor of Civil Engineering, 1972–93. During Sabbatical leave, 1974 – 75, he was visiting Professor at Cornell University and at the University of Washington. On his retirement in 1993, he was made Professor Emeritus in Civil Engineering.

His areas of research which established him as a giant in Civil Engineering included: Reinforced Concrete Structures; Model Analysis of Structures; Dynamics of Structures; Development of Highway Bridge Systems, Pre–stressed Laminated Wood Bridge.

His community involvement included: extensive involvement in community activities on issues of Race Relations, Community Policing and Human Rights. Dr Batchelor received many honours including: Distinguished Service Award, Queen's University, Reviewed in 'Who's Who in America;' 'Who's Who in Canada.'